SpringerBriefs in Public Health

SpringerBriefs in Public Health present concise summaries of cutting-edge research and practical applications from across the entire field of public health, with contributions from medicine, bioethics, health economics, public policy, biostatistics, and sociology.

The focus of the series is to highlight current topics in public health of interest to a global audience, including health care policy; social determinants of health; health issues in developing countries; new research methods; chronic and infectious disease epidemics; and innovative health interventions.

Featuring compact volumes of 50 to 125 pages, the series covers a range of content from professional to academic. Possible volumes in the series may consist of timely reports of state-of-the art analytical techniques, reports from the field, Snapshots of hot and/or emerging topics, elaborated theses, literature reviews, and in-depth case studies. Both solicited and unsolicited manuscripts are considered for publication in this series.

Briefs are published as part of Springer's eBook collection, with millions of users worldwide. In addition, Briefs are available for individual print and electronic purchase.

Briefs are characterized by fast, global electronic dissemination, standard publishing contracts, easy-to-use manuscript preparation and formatting guidelines, and expedited production schedules. We aim for publication 8–12 weeks after acceptance.

More information about this series at http://www.springer.com/series/10138

A. L. Hamdan

Strategic Thinking in a Hospital Setting

 Springer

A. L. Hamdan
Department of Otolaryngology
American University of Beirut Medical
    Center
Beirut
Lebanon

ISSN 2192-3698   ISSN 2192-3701   (electronic)
SpringerBriefs in Public Health
ISBN 978-3-319-53596-8   ISBN 978-3-319-53597-5   (eBook)
DOI 10.1007/978-3-319-53597-5

Library of Congress Control Number: 2017932084

Printed on acid-free paper

This Springer imprint is published by Springer Nature
The registered company is Springer International Publishing AG
The registered company address is: Gewerbestrasse 11, 6330 Cham, Switzerland

*I dedicate this book to my parents Hussein
and Jamila Hamdan with warm gratitude
for their inspiration and guidance
&
To my wife Sawsan for her relentless support
and enchanting smile.*

Preface

The healthcare system is facing numerous challenges. These include the explosion in scientific knowledge, the link of pay to performance, and, most importantly, the shift to "patient-centered" care approach. Attempts to circumvent these challenges and improve on the quality of care have been invariably mitigated by a prohibitive rising cost. All the aforementioned has fostered a transition in the understanding and delivery of health care from an industrial economical view that focuses on services and products as outcome measures to a modern view that highlights the importance of customer's perception and experience as determinants of quality of care provision.

This transition in the healthcare industry mandates the adoption of a strategic plan that anticipates the dynamic changes in patient's needs and the rising cost in the provision of those needs. Physicians in administrative positions and managers have to acquire and develop different types of strategies commonly used in health care and other industries in order to maintain their financial viability and defend their market's share. To this end, this book is intended to equip physicians and administrators with the right strategic tools and frameworks. The focus of this book is on the different strategic directions commonly adopted by strategist in different industries. The different strategic views conceptualized in health care in addition to a crafted strategic framework that can be used to draw a summary of the market competitive dynamics will be described. Once the strategist has chosen the strategic direction for its firm, a strategic plan must follow. The application of the most common strategies used in other industries to develop and sustain a competitive advantage will be discussed with special focus on Porter's strategies, namely low-cost leadership and service differentiation. These strategies have been described thoroughly in the literature as dominant typologies adopted by many firms in various industries; however, few are the reports on the application of these strategies in hospital settings. In the last two chapters, this book highlights the application of Porter's strategies in a set of Lebanese hospitals with emphasis on the limitations, constraints, and correlation factors between types of strategies used and performance of these hospitals. Last but not least, eight strategic tactics will be discussed thoroughly with special attention to the operational initiatives, indicators, and goals of each.

Beirut, Lebanon   A. L. Hamdan

Contents

About the Author

A. L. Hamdan is currently a Professor of Otolaryngology—Head and Neck Surgery, Head of Division of Laryngology and Director of "Hamdan Voice Unit" at the American University of Beirut Medical Center (AUBMC). He holds an Executive Master's in Business Administration from The American University of Beirut, a Master's degree in Health Science and a Master's degree in Hospital Administration from École Supérieure Des Affaires, in addition to a Diploma in Strategy and Innovation from Oxford University.

He is the founder and director of the "Hamdan Voice Unit" at AUBMC, founder and president of the "Lebanese Voice Association" and the "Voice Foundation Lebanon Chapter", with 120 publications in refereed journals in the field of Voice and Laryngology. Following his position as Chairperson of the Faculty Development Committee for two years, during which he promoted the business aspect of medicine through the organization of numerous workshops in collaboration with the Olayan School of Business, he assumed the position of Medical Director of Strategy and Innovation at AUBMC where he has been engaged in the assessment and development of strategic initiatives.

Abbreviations

AHRQ   Agency for Healthcare Research and Quality
HCAHPS   Hospital Consumer Assessment of Healthcare Providers and Systems
NHS   National Health Service
NQF   National Quality Forum

Chapter 1
Introduction

The Health Care System is facing numerous challenges. These include the explosion in scientific knowledge, the link of pay to performance, and most importantly the shift to "Patient Centered Care" approach. Attempts to circumvent these challenges and improve on the quality of care have been invariably mitigated by a prohibitive rising cost. The healthcare expenditure estimated to be $26 billion in 2003 has exceeded one sixth of the GDP in the United States [1] and is still draining the economy with an increase to 2.97 trillion in 2014 [2] Similarly, the rise in health care expenditure in 2014 has reached the figures of $271.99 trillion in the United Kingdom and $14.382 billion in the United Arab of Emirates accounting for 3.6% of its annual budget. Add to this exuberate cost is the frequency of medical errors which represents the eighth leading cause of death with 98,000 mortalities a year from medical errors in the United States [3].

That being said, the healthcare system is in crisis. It has failed to meet patient's expectations with more than 40 million people having no medical coverage in the United States. Based on "Crossing the Quality Chasm" by the Institute of Medicine, "—the nation's healthcare delivery system has fallen far short in its ability to translate knowledge into practice and to apply new technology safely and appropriately" [4]. These shortcomings in healthcare delivery were brought further to light with the public reporting of healthcare measures by the "Hospital Consumers Assessment of Healthcare Providers and Systems (HCAHPS)", and the public expression of views on medical service, an act that was formally endorsed by the National Quality Forum (NQF) in 2015 [5]. All the aforementioned has fostered a transition in the understanding and delivery of healthcare from an industrial economical view that focuses on services and products as outcome measures to a modern view that highlights the importance of customer's perception and experience as determinants of quality in care provision. It has set ground for a new phase in healthcare described by the National Health Service (NHS) as the "Next Stage" with high quality care for all [6]. In this stage, pay became linked to performance as stated by the Affordable Care Act, and patient's reported measures of care became critical to Pay and performance [7]. To this end, many cross cutting patient-reported

© The Author(s) 2017
A. L. Hamdan, *Strategic Thinking in a Hospital Setting*,
SpringerBriefs in Public Health, DOI 10.1007/978-3-319-53597-5_1

measures have been described and these include patient satisfaction, patient perception, patient participation and patient preferences. Despite the complexity in the definition of patient's engagement, there is a unanimous agreement on the constructs that need to be incorporated in the healthcare reform plan, with emphasis on clinical and managerial quality.

This transition in the healthcare industry with the focus on quality in patient's care mandates the adoption of a 'Strategic Plan' that anticipates the dynamic changes in patient's needs and the rising cost in the provision of those needs. Given the high degree of interdependence in the current global economy, hospitals after thorough examination of the various industry profitability and growth, must position themselves in the right market, be it primary, secondary or tertiary care. Once in the proper strategic position, the corresponding resources must be allocated and capabilities must be exploited towards the delivery of better services and the development of new offerings. To this end, knowledge exploitation and the availability of resources for innovation must lead to technological advances, a major attribute that challenges all healthcare providers who wish to remain at the forefront in medical care.

Similarly, given the blurred boundaries of Physician's role in Hospital settings, medical practitioners, from their own conceptual term, must also properly position themselves in the right industry. This can be any venue in the healthcare arena, including third party providers and pharmaceutical companies. In order to gain competitive advantage, physicians in key administrative or leadership positions must reinvent themselves to meet the changes in healthcare. A shift in value from salaried employee to strategic thinkers must take place in order to better manage the global market in healthcare. This mandates enhancement of Physicians' strategic competencies in addition to their leadership, managerial and communication skills. Again, once rightly positioned, they need to allocate their own resources to achieve the strategic goals intended. The resources can be personal such as inherent competencies, tacit information and business acumen, or financial. If properly cultivated into capabilities of strategic relevance, these resources can help achieve not only individual goals as mentioned previously but also the vision and mission of their medical institution at large. For this reason, proper alignment of both physicians and administrators interest through the development of physician integration programs and strong liaison between the two is crucial for the success of any strategy.

Given the constantly growing needs in healthcare and the increasing challenges of globalization, there is rarely uniformity in the vision of the various staff and faculty within a medical organization. The discrepancy between the vision embraced by the leader and the actual stand of the organization creates tension and assumptions. A good strategist will convert these assumptions to values and will capitalize on the discrepancy between factuality and expectations to gear the energy of all staff and physicians towards that vision. By drawing a concrete image of the organization's goals and objectives, embracing that image by all the key players, and allocating resources towards the achievement of these goals, strategists can succeed in sailing the organization to its right destination.

That being said, this book will focus on the different strategic directions commonly adopted by strategist in different industries. The different Strategic views conceptualized in healthcare in addition to a crafted strategic framework that can be used to draw a summary of the market competitive dynamics will be described. Once the strategist has chosen the strategic direction for its firm, a strategic plan must follow. The application of the most common strategies used in other industries to develop and sustain a competitive advantage will be discussed with special focus on Porter's strategies, namely Low cost leadership and service differentiation. Last but not least eight strategic tactics will be discussed thoroughly with special attention to the operational initiatives, indicators and goals of each.

In the last two chapters I will highlight the application of Porter's strategies in a set of Lebanese Hospitals with emphasis on the limitations, constraints and correlation factors between types of strategies used and performance of these hospitals.

References

1. Herzlinger, R. E., 2006. Why Innovation in Health Care is so Hard. In: no ed. 2011.
2. Xu, K., Evans, D.B., Kawabata, K., Zeramdini, R., Klavus, J. and Murray, C.J., 2003. Household catastrophic health expenditure: a multicountry analysis. *The lancet, 362*(9378), pp. 111–117. Available at: http://data.worldbank.org/indicator/SH.XPD.TOTL.ZS.
3. Spear, S. J., 2005. Fixing Health Care from the Inside, Today. In: no ed. 2011. *Harvard Business Review Fixing Health Care From Inside & Out.* Boston, Massachusetts: Harvard Business Review Press. pp. 49–90.
4. Institute of Medicine, 2001. Crossing the Quality Chasm: A New Health System for the 21st Century. Washington, DC: National Academies Press.
5. HCAHPS, 2015. Hospital consumer's assessment of healthcare providers and systems. [online] Available at: http://www.hcahpsonline.org/home.aspx [Accessed 14 January 2015].
6. Department of Health. 2008. High Quality Care For All: NHS Next Stage Review Final Report [online]. Available at: https://www.gov.uk/government/uploads/system/uploads/attachment_data/file/228836/7432.pdf [Accessed 14 January 2015].
7. Hofer, A.N., Abraham, J. and Moscovice, I., 2011. Expansion of coverage under the Patient Protection and Affordable Care Act and primary care utilization. *Milbank Quarterly, 89*(1), pp. 69–89. Available at: http://www.dpc.senate.gov/healthreformbill/healthbill04.pdf [Accessed 14 January 2015].

Chapter 2
Strategic Directions and Views

Once the goals and objectives of an enterprise have been set, different strategic views and directions ought to be solicited in attempt to meet those goals. Two main views are traditionally used in any industry and these include the positional view and the resource based view [1].

In the *Positional view*, strategic planning primarily lies in envisioning the position of a given healthcare provider in the healthcare arena whether it is a primary care or tertiary care provider. The strategist tries to answer the question "where do we stand, what is our market share, and how can we defend it?". The main Competitive advantage of the firm or hospital is its current position in the market with the industry structure being the arena for competition. In this perspective marketing information system is often deployed as a competitive advantage and used to determine the hospital market share and position. This fact mandates proper understanding of the various industry's attributes as well as the competitive forces that shape the position of the firm and its long term profitability [2]. The main Industry attributes that are analyzed are the rate of growth and profitability, geographic accessibility, strategic alliances, in addition to the weight and impact of technological innovation on its performance.

In the healthcare industry both growth and technological advances carry significant weight on the Performance of healthcare providers. A fast growing industry is inclined to empower both suppliers and consumers. This is attributed to the demographic changes, advances in research and explosion in medical knowledge at large. Demographically, the increase in the overall world population in parallel with the increase in the average lifespan puts the healthcare industry on a fast growing track with growing demands such as the need for geriatric medical facilities, home care centers and palliative medicine. Similarly, the Technological advances have an impactful role on the growth and profitability of healthcare providers. In the healthcare industry at large and in hospital settings in particular, technological growth is key in providing medical care. Hospitals that assume a forefront position in the health care arena have to ensure a constant stream of financial and human resources to maintain their technological advancement, which in turn challenges

© The Author(s) 2017
A. L. Hamdan, *Strategic Thinking in a Hospital Setting*,
SpringerBriefs in Public Health, DOI 10.1007/978-3-319-53597-5_2

administrators who are keen on providing state of the art diagnostic and therapeutic regimens. On the other hand, when technological advancement is slow, the impact of technological shifts on medical practice is little. This is more commonly seen in primary care facilities or practice in rural areas.

Of equal importance to the industry attributes is the ecosystem which allows the success or failure of a firm's complementary products and services [3]. Example is the role of governmental rules and regulations in healthcare which plays a tremendous role in the insurgence of new competitors such as new hospital facilities and or in fostering the expansion of existing capacities, such as the increase in the number of beds within a hospital. Other examples of Complementary products in healthcare are the means for financial and geographic accessibility to medical services, availability of accessary and adjunctive therapeutic services such as physical therapy following major head and neck surgery.

Once the aforementioned industry attributes have been examined, the strategic analyst in his positional view must dissect Porter's five forces in order to estimate Industry profitability and the rivalry among the existing competitors [4]. The major competitive forces include the "threat of entry", the "power of suppliers", the "power of the customer", the "threat of substitute" and "rivalry among existing competitors" [4].

The threat of entry is intimately related to capital cost requirement, the demand side benefits of scale, and or customer/patient switching cost, in addition to restrictions imposed by governmental policies such as trading barriers, emergence of new laws and patents [4]. In healthcare provision, invariably a large capital is needed as a start, which makes the threat of entry low, especially if the local healthcare policies deter the development of new healthcare facilities. This threat is further deterred by constraints in the healthcare budget. Patient loyalty is also a crucial fact when new threats are in surge. This latter can be enhanced thru the availability of electronic medical record and the accessibility of patients to medical information. The threat of entry also depends on incumbency advantages in terms of cumulative experience and competencies, access to distribution channels, and economy of scale from the supply side. A fifty year old medical center with inherent competencies in terms of processes, flow of patients and flow of information, in addition to a strong network with physicians and neighboring healthcare providers, must have a strong position in the market and thus raises the barriers to entry.

Customers may also exert tremendous power. By customer we are obviously referring to patients who can often exert pressure on hospitals and medical centers especially if they are self-payers. Patient's power can also be derived from group purchasing as seen in compacts made by selected groups, usually of similar profession, and hospitals. A low switching cost exemplified by the presence of nearby competitors, the lack of differentiated services secondary to insufficient resources and expertise, and the ability of customers to integrate backward are also factors that strengthen patient's position in the healthcare chain. The ability to integrate backward is often exemplified when insurance companies buy group practices and consolidate with hospitals in attempt to control cost and exert pressure on health-care providers.

Substitutes can also represent a threat and limit the profitability of hospitals by reducing their dominance in the market as well. Again this is more prominent when medical services lack differentiation and or branding. Substitutes for conventional medicine can include acupuncture, homeopathic therapy, cognitive therapy, meditation, Chinese medicine and biologically based therapies [5]. These alternatives or complementary medical therapies will not be the subject of discussion in this chapter, but suffices to say that these need to be considered as threats given the cultural context and environment.

Last but not least is market rivalry among existing competitors. This latter is more precipitated in the presence of numerous competitors with almost even powers and when the industry growth is low. When Growth in healthcare is slow, hospitals can turn aggressive in order to either maintain their market share or increase their profitability. The competition becomes fiercer when the exit barriers are high making it very hard and non-lucrative for competitors to leave.

Once the industry attributes have been examined and the competitive forces have been understood with all their underpinning, the role of the strategist is to properly position the firm or hospital vis-à-vis its competitors in the market, to anticipate possible shifts in the market, and to exploit the expected industry changes in attempt to identify emerging opportunities and claim new strategic position. The strategist should also shape the industry structure by reacting to the competitive forces in a constructive manner [6]. In healthcare two examples can be given; one is value constellation and two is Game theory. In value constellation the role of all the key players is reconfigured in order to add value to the end product. The conventional role of each is re-examined in attempt to provide a better product or service [7]. In the supply to purchasing (S2P) project, where suppliers, surgeons and purchasing are the key players, surgeons are invited to examine the most common surgical supplies used with the purpose of optimizing utilization and cost. Engaging physicians in the design and utilization of supplies is an example of value constellation and value addition. Another example of reacting to the competitive forces is the value net strategic frame by Brandenburger and Nalebuff [8]. In any game the essence of a win-win relation lies in the provision of an added value to the end product or service by all the key players. By looking at the position of all the stakeholders and using an allocentric rather than egocentric perspective, the cooperative as well as the competitive nature of any game is enhanced. This value net strategic framework highlights the interdependence of the participants in healthcare provision, namely the patient, physician, medical staff and third party players, while emphasizing the strong interaction between them. So in order to create value within this framework identification of the major players and the understanding of the basic rules of the game is crucial.

Another equally important strategic view in addition to the positional view is the *Resource based view*. In this view the strategist looks within the institution at its resources and capabilities in attempt to develop new competencies that are of strategic relevance [9]. The main question to be answered is "What are we good at" and how can we leverage on our competencies to expand our market share and grow further. This view is more commonly adopted in unstable environments characterized by turmoil that makes industry attractiveness an elusive strategic start [10]. Instead, the firm's bundle of resources and capabilities are exploited in a strategic competitive manner. The resources, defined as "the productive assets of a firm" can be either tangible such as properties and equipment or intangible such as branding, reputation and tacit information embedded in routinization and processes. Capabilities on the other hand are the way resources are deployed in a constructive manner towards the achievement of a desired end result. These can be classified either on a functional basis thru the identification of various capabilities within the different functional units of the institution, or based on a value chain analysis of the main activities undertaken by that institution. An example of a capability within a functional unit is the diagnostic yield in the department of radiology. The imaging equipment considered as resources are deployed in a successful manner thru the radiology staff to generate a major capability that carries a high diagnostic yield. Similarly, if we were to examine the value chain activities in the work up of a patient with chest pain, the Fast flow of information and efficient management in the emergency department may be considered as major capabilities. In both cases, it is important to note that for a capability to be of strategic relevance it must generate a competitive advantage through proper exploitation of its corresponding competencies.

References

1. Peteraf, M.A., 1993. The cornerstones of competitive advantage: a resource-based view. *Strategic management journal*, *14*(3), pp. 179–191.
2. Miller, D., 1988. Relating Porter's business strategies to environment and structure: Analysis and performance implications. *Academy of management Journal*, *31*(2), pp. 280–308.
3. Adner, R., 2006. Match your innovation strategy to your innovation ecosystem. *Harvard business review*, *84*(4), p. 98.
4. Porter, M.E., 2008. "The five competitive forces that shape strategy". Harvard Business Review 57 (January 2008):57–71 Porter five forces.
5. Swierzewski, S. J., MD. (2001, January 01). Traditional Chinese Medicine Overview. Retrieved September 05, 2016. Available at: www.healthcommunities.com/...chinese-medicine/alternative-medicine/tcm-treatments.shtml.
6. Porter, ME. (2007), *Understanding Industry Structure*, Harvard Business School note #9-707-493.
7. Normann, R. and Ramírez, R. (1993), 'From Value Chain to Value Constellation: Designing Interactive Strategy', *Harvard Business Review*, 71(4): 65–77.
8. Brandenburger, AM. and Nalebuff, BJ. (1995), 'The Right Game: Use Game Theory to Shape Strategy', *Harvard Business Review*, 73(4): 57–71.
9. Porter, M., 1980. Competitive Strategy. New York: Free Press.
10. Miller, D., and Friesen, P.H., 1984. *Organizations: A Quantum View*. New Jersey: Prentice-Hall ref on resource based view being more suitable in unstable environment.

Chapter 3
Porter's Strategies in Healthcare

Healthcare delivery has undergone a dramatic reform over the last few decades. It has witnessed a paradigm shift where patient's satisfaction has become critical. Patient empowerment has transformed healthcare into a value based business where physicians and healthcare providers are challenged to meet the emerging needs of patients in a dynamic market constrained by financial resources and governed by the challenges of the global business environment.

> On one hand hospitals need to remain at the forefront in the provision of state of the art medical care using high technology imaging and unique services, on the other hand they have to undergo radical cost transformation in view of the diminished budget for healthcare both in the private and public sectors.

Cemented to these hurdles, and in consequence to the aforementioned transformation, there have been a large number of consolidations among hospitals in attempt to maintain their financial stability and expand their market share. As a result, the healthcare system in the United States has witnessed more than 900 merges between hospitals [1]. Despite the large number of mergers and acquisitions, there was still fierce competition among hospitals with deep concern on the rise in prices and the quality of care that is delivered [2]. Subsequently, healthcare managers have adopted different types of strategy, the most common of which are low cost leadership and service differentiation [3].

According to Porter these two types of strategies can be further categorized into four depending on the market segment and niche where the strategy is implemented, be it a narrow segment of the market or the market as a whole [3]. In the first scenario where cost leadership is used in a focused or well defined market segment, the strategy is referred to as a focused cost leadership strategy whereas when differentiation is used in a focused market segment, the strategy is referred to as focused differentiation strategy. The hybrid form, combining low cost leadership with service differentiation, has been most challenging to managers who aim at quality care and cost reduction.

© The Author(s) 2017
A. L. Hamdan, *Strategic Thinking in a Hospital Setting*,
SpringerBriefs in Public Health, DOI 10.1007/978-3-319-53597-5_3

3.1   Choice of Strategy

The application of Porter's generic strategies in the hospital industry has been proven to be useful despite the scarcity in the reports [4, 5]. Both types of strategy, namely cost leadership strategy and differentiation strategy in their focused and broad applications have been used to coop with the changes in healthcare environment.

There are only two reports on the applicability of Porter's strategies in healthcare, one by Kumar et al. on the United States hospitals and the other by Hlavacka et al. on Slovak hospital industry [4, 5]. The first study by Kumar et al. performed on 600 acute care hospitals looked at the types of strategies used by chief administrators and how these strategies correlated with performance. Five groups of strategies have been reported and traditional performance criteria were used as measure of organizational performance. The five types of strategies included cost leaders, differentiators, stuck in the middle, focused cost leaders and focused differentiators. With respect to performance, return on new services and facilities, ability to retain patients and to control expenditure, were used as measures of effectiveness and efficiency. The second study by Hlavacka et al. was conducted on Slovak hospitals using a translated version of Kumar's questionnaire. Again their findings indicated four types of strategy, namely the Focused cost leadership, the stuck in the middle, the "wait and see group" which had medium emphasis on cost leadership and low emphasis on focus and differentiation, and last but not least is cost leadership. The results showed that the "stuck in the middle" performed better that the remaining groups.

The use of differentiation strategy has been linked and attributed to the presence of discontinuous or turbulent environments which invariably favor the adoption of a differentiation strategy. According to the resource-based view [6], looking inside the firm's resources and capabilities is the cornerstone for differentiation strategy in a market that is unpredictable and discontinuous. Despite that several studies support the notion of Porter's generic strategies' applicability and viability in different environmental contexts [7, 8], many others have emphasized the importance of fitting the organizational strategy with environmental conditions [9, 10]. The discontinuous environment in healthcare can be characterized by surges in technology, introduction of new payment's method, unforeseen patients' needs, healthcare business restructuring, last but not least are political conflicts which always had an impact on the overall socio-economic status among which is healthcare expenditure.

The lack of pursuit of differentiation strategy on the other hand can be attributed to several factors: One is the limited resources and scarcity in funding. Based on numerous studies [11, 12], differentiation mandates funding and significant resources, the lack of which can circumvent the establishment of new services and the ability to enhance current ones. Asides from having access to research funds and endowments primarily used in academic institutions, private and non-academic hospitals are at a disadvantage in terms of financial resources as the cut down in healthcare budgeting had affected the overall expenditure and reduced allocation of resources used in differentiation of existing medical services [13, 14]. The second reason why hospitals may not adopt a differentiation strategy is the type and mode of reimbursement. When pay is based on contractual agreements between hospitals and third party payers, with a fixed amount allocated for the management of disease entities, there is less of an incentive to spend on differentiation of medical facilities, unless reimbursement is also linked to patient experience or other intermediate healthcare outcome measures [15]. A third Reason for missing on differentiation strategy is lack of a market information system. Based on a study by Narver [16], institutions that are market oriented tend to adopt more differentiation strategy. This inclination stems from the urge to meet patient's needs and emerging quests. Institutions that follow closely the market and what patients want tend to differentiate their services from both the demand side and the supply side as well. In developing countries "Utilizing market research to identify new services" is rarely used.

That being said, Cost leadership has been more advocated in stable environments where competitive forces and threats are rather predictable, whereas differentiation strategy has been more advised in unpredictable and dynamic environments. A main reason to adopt the low cost leadership is the nature of the payer mix, that is when the majority of patients are insured by third party payers and only a small fraction pay for their medical fees. In this case, most of the hospital bill is covered or reimbursed by insurance companies. Based on a report by Newhouse [17] on "the structure of the health insurance and the erosion of the medical market place" insured patients are less inclined to search for the lowest prices in seeking medical care. From the supply side, hospitals tend to compete less on price and more on differentiation to attract patients. This has been referred to as the "medical arms race" by Robinson and Luft [18] where hospitals try to attract patients by widening the breadth of their products or by introducing new services rather than by reducing cost. Focusing on differentiation when the price is fixed is in accordance with numerous reports on non-price competition that were described in other industries, such as the airline industry [19, 20].

3.1.1 Cost Leadership Strategy

To be a cost leader means to be the lowest cost producer in the industry. The competitive advantage is derived from widening the gap between the cost of production and what the customer is willing to pay [7]. This entails Minimization of cost in various operational fields, business restructuring and revamping of the overall cost structure.

Different approaches to reduce cost have been described in the literature. One basic approach is catalog activity with value chain analysis [21]. All the services within a department are dissected and evaluated in terms of cost. Using catalog activities, each service is disintegrated into a set of activities where the importance and cost of each is analyzed in relation to the overall cost and in relation to the customer's need and market segment. The cost drivers are identified and analyzed in terms of opportunities for outsourcing or reallocation in order to reduce the overall cost. The market cost drivers are used as a benchmark for cost management. Redundancies, duplications in services and wasteful expenditures are reexamined. Not essential activities are either outsourced or re-allocated. A relevant product for catalog activity analysis in healthcare setting is the hospital bill. This latter is usually stratified into room and service, use of supplies, pharmaceuticals, diagnostic tests, and operating room in case a surgical procedure has been done. The cost drivers would be the length of stay, the choice of surgical supplies used, the variety of diagnostic tests requested, and last but not least the duration of surgery. By dissecting these cost drivers in relation to the consensual figures in the market, one can identify how financial resources are being spent and how cost can be reduced.

Another approach for low cost leadership is cost management in the different segments or departments of an institution. Based on Michael E. Rindler book on strategic cost reduction [22] cost is dissected along six dimensions; Management cost, supply cost, labor cost, service cost, utilization cost and capital cost. In each dimension, different strategic tools can be used. Hence several strategic areas for cost reduction starting from inbound logistics to marketing and sale should be contemplated. With respect to input cost, a decrease in cost can be realized using economy of scale whereas in the production phase, cost reduction can be reached by re-engineering the business processes and improving the quality of the products or services. Economies of learning can also assist in cost reduction by improving the agility at the individual level and the global know how at the institutional level. In marketing and sale, proper matching between customer needs and service/product supply is crucial in retaining customers and sustaining loyalty.

In a hospital setting, the biggest challenge is to reduce cost without jeopardizing the quality of care or the range of services. For cost reduction to be successful it must be aligned with the overall strategy of the institution and must engage all levels of management including physicians and staff. This requires integration between the different key players in order to enhance the flow of patients, information and hence care. Inability to engage physicians and or poor alignment with the institutional vision invariably leads to failure.

Whereas economies of learning by enhancing the know-how and dexterity of care givers, by designing services that are easy to deliver, and by improving the clinical utilization of the hospital resources and capabilities, can result in cost reduction and lead to success.

With respect to sales and marketing, it is about meeting patient's expectations and keeping the promise of delivering the best services at an affordable cost. While keeping this promise, the hospital is ensuring good visibility to its staff and caring team. There are several examples to cost reduction in hospital settings and these include: merging and acquisition, staff layoff, supply chain management, reducing waste, outsourcing and insourcing of given services, reducing the layers in management, capital cost management, and so forth.

3.1.2 Differentiation Strategy

With respect to differentiation, by definition it is about the provision of a service or a product with distinctive attributes that are of added value to the customer [3]. It is not just about being different but about matching the needs of the customer and sustaining these needs in a cost-effective manner. This entails proper understanding and dissection of the two facets of this interface, namely the customer's perspective of what is needed and what is factually being provided by the supplier. Hence, we need to analyze the decision making process of the customer and his journey in converting his needs into demands and wants, and we need to meet this latter by tailoring the process of service or product delivery. That being said, differentiation can be from the demand side and the supplier side. In healthcare, differentiation is about meeting patient's needs by providing patient centered care with state of the art technology and expertise (Supply side).

Different approaches for differentiation have been described in the literature, all of which converge towards the provision of better quality of service and patient experience. The first approach is by improving the level of offering vis-à-vis the key success factors in the industry of healthcare [23]. This starts by identifying the key success factors that cover the different points of intersection along the patient's continuum of care starting from the search for information to the time of visit and follow up. The various key success factors in the healthcare industry and their level of offering by the institution are displayed graphically. These may include the accessibility to service, geographic location, religious background, mode, date and time of appointment, greeting of staff, waiting time, paper work, time spent with physician, diagnostic yield and follow up with patients. This graphic display will allow the strategist to visualize and portray the performance of his/her institution vis-à-vis the various external and internal aforementioned key success factors. This is followed by proper selection and exploitation of the variables considered of strategic relevance in a fashion that enables differentiation of the existing services. Differentiation is then implemented along those key strategic variables in order to improve patient care.

Differentiation can also be implemented by improving the final or intermediate outcome measures in healthcare. It can be gaged by the extent to which healthcare providers succeed in preventing disease, improving quality of life and reducing mortality. In can also be weighed vis-à-vis its performance towards the six intermediate outcome measures, namely quality, efficiency, utilization, accessibility, learning and sustainability [24]. As previously mentioned differentiation of hospital services can have several dimensions to it at different points of intersection with the patient's continuum of care. The differentiation can be in improving access to the healthcare providers, widening the range of the services provided and engaging in a unique service of added value. Other venues for differentiation include having state of the art technology and competent staff. Providing patient's support thru patient's affair office that follow-up on patient's needs and care is also a major feature of differentiation. The differentiation of these key success factors will ultimately lead to better intermediate outcome measures and better quality of life.

The second approach in differentiation strategy is selecting the most important services and performing activity analysis in terms of differentiation [21]. This Catalog activity helps in identifying the drivers for uniqueness in each activity. These are then linked to the overall value drivers of a given healthcare provider and ultimately to the patient's needs. The purpose is to identify the added value of each activity within a given service and the means by which it contributes to a better outcome. This value chain analysis allows the strategist to examine thoroughly each activity's attributes within a service, explore new options and derive new choices. As such a thorough view of all the possible matches between the existing capabilities of the institution and the patient's needs are analyzed in order to exceed patient's expectations. In other terms, the focus is on the exploitation of the current capabilities and core competencies of the institution with the purpose of developing and sustaining a competitive advantage that can lead to better quality of care.

> In both aforementioned described approaches, the purpose is to differentiate the existing services and or to create new services. Questions such as "Have you introduced new services", "Have you differentiated the existing services" and or "Have you used market research to identify new services" can be used to identify hospitals that adopt the differentiation strategy.

References

1. Jaklevic, M., 2002. Tired trend. *Modern Healthcare,* 32 (26), 10.
2. Gaynor, M. Haas-Wilson, D., 1999. Change, consolidation, and competition in health care markets. *J Econ Perspect.,* 13(1), pp. 141–164.
3. Porter's (1980) generic strategies as determinants of strategic group membership and organizational performance. *Academy of Management journal, 27*(3), pp. 467–488. Available at: Porter's Generic Competitive Strategies (ways of competing) www.ifm.eng.cam.ac.uk/.../ porters-generic-competitive-strategies/.
4. Hlavacka, S., Bacharova, L., Rusnakova, V., Wagner, R., 2001. Performance implications of Porter's generic strategies in Slovak hospitals. *Journal of Management in Medicine,* 15(1), pp. 44–66.
5. Kumar, K., Subramanian, R., Yauger, C., 1997. Pure versus hybrid: performance implications of Porter's generic strategies. *Health Care Management Review,* 22(4), pp. 47–60.
6. Grant, R. M. (2013). *Contemporary Strategy Analysis, 8th Edition* (8th ed.). Wiley.
7. Porter, M., 1980. Competitive Strategy. New York: Free Press.
8. Miles, R. E., & Snow, C. C. 1978. *Organizational Strategy, Structure, and Process*. New York: McGraw-Hill.
9. Kim, L., and Lim, Y., 1988. Environment, Generic Strategies, and Performance in a Rapidly Developing Country: A Taxonomic Approach. *Academy of Management journal,* 31, 10. 2307/256339.
10. Miller, D., 1988. Relating Porter's Business Strategies to Environment and Structure: Analysis and Performance Implications. *Academy of Management Journal,* 31 (2), 280–308.

11. Zelman, W.A., 1996. *The Changing Health Care Marketplace.* San Francisco, CA: Private Ventures, Public Interests, Jossey-Bass Publishers.
12. Trinh, H.Q., 1999. Are rural hospitals 'strategic'? *Health Care Management Review,* 24 (3), pp. 42–54.
13. Derhally, M., 2010. Lebanon Cabinet Approves 2010 Draft Budget, First in Five Years. Bloomberg business week, [online] 18 June. Available at: http://www.bloomberg.com/news/2010-06-18/lebanon-cabinet-approves-first-budget-in-five-years-amid-rising-deficit.html [Accessed 19 January 2015].
14. *Ammar, W., 2009. Health beyond politics. Beirut. World Health Organization/Ministry of Public Health.*
15. Ammar, W., 2003. *Health system and reform in Lebanon.*Beyrouth, Liban: Entreprise Universitaire d'Etudes et de Publications – B. P. 1136311.
16. Narver, J.C., and Slater, S.F., 1990. The Effect of Market Orientation on Business Profitability. *Journal of Marketing,* 54, 20–35.
17. Newhouse, J.P., 1978. The structure of health insurance and the erosion of the medical marketplace. In: Greenberg, W., ed. Competetion in the Health Care Sector: Past, Present, and Future. Germantown, MD: Aspen Publishers.
18. Robinson, J.C., Luft, H., 1985. The impact of hospital market structure on patient volume, average length of stay, and the cost of care. *Journal of Health Economics,* 4, pp. 333–56.
19. Douglas, GW. and Miller, JC., 1974. Quality competition, industry equilibrium, and efficiency in the price-constrained airline market, *The American Economic Review],* 64(4), pp. 657–69.
20. White, L.J. 1972. Quality Variation When Price are Regulated. *The Bell Journal of Economics and Management Science,* 3(2): pp. 425–436.
21. Ghemawat, P and Rivkin, J.W. 2006. Creating competitive advantage: Harvard business school Background Note 798-062, January 1998.
22. Rindler, M.E, 2006.Why do Some Hospitals Fail? In: J. Davis, A. Bove, C. Underdown, eds. 2006. *Strategic Cost Reduction, Leading Your Hospital to Success.* North Franklin Street, Chicago: Health Administration Press. Ch.3.
23. Mark Hollingworth, 2012. McGill Executive Institute.
24. McKee, M., Figueras, J., & Saltman, R. B. (2011). *Health Systems, Health, Wealth And Societal Well-Being: Assessing The Case For Investing In Health Systems: Assessing the case for investing in health systems.* McGraw-Hill Education (UK).

Chapter 4
Sources of Competitive Advantage

A hospital possesses a competitive advantage over its rivals when it either earns a higher profit in the provision of an equally differentiated service/product as its competitors, or when it distinguishes itself with an added value service compared to its competitors. The first type of competitive advantage would stem obviously from low cost leadership whereas the second type stems from service differentiation strategy [1, 2]. Either one is the byproduct of imperfection in the availability of healthcare resources [3]. These can be in relation to market segment, technology, human resources, and or strategic alliances. In relation to market segments, imperfections can be dependent on demographic variables or simply issues of accessibility, be it geographic, linguistic or financial. Uneven availability of advanced technology is another form of resource imperfection that can put one hospital at a competitive disadvantage versus others. Similarly strategic networks and significant affiliations may be limited to one competitor thus giving him a major competitive advantage. That being said, there are two sources for a competitive advantage: One external and the other internal [4, 5]. External sources can be secondary to demographic changes, as mentioned previously such as the increase in the geriatric population, to dynamic changes in the market such as the emergence of new segment, or to the presence of new substitutes. Other external sources include change in payer mix, acquisitions and merging of medical centers, and last but not least is change in pricing which can lead to war of prices. The presence of heterogeneity in resources is not enough for an external source to be an effective basis of competitive advantage for a healthcare provider. This latter must react to these resources in a constructive and strategic manner. For a competitive advantage to develop, rapid response and allocation of resources to a given opportunity is a mandate [6].

The other sources of competitive advantage are the internal resources which are based primarily on incremental and radical innovation [7]. In the healthcare sector, innovation can be in the attributes of a medical service, in the medical information system, and or in the accessibility of patients to their medical files. An innovative process engineering that results in increased process efficiency pertaining patient

© The Author(s) 2017
A. L. Hamdan, *Strategic Thinking in a Hospital Setting*,
SpringerBriefs in Public Health, DOI 10.1007/978-3-319-53597-5_4

flow, technology be it diagnostic and/or advanced such as the PET scan or thera-peutic such as In Vitro-Fertilization, is obviously an internal source of competitive advantage. Another internal source for a competitive advantage lies in targeting nascent markets or creating new ones which is one of the pure forms of Blue Ocean Strategy [8]. Example is creating the need for cosmetic surgery secondary to an increase in awareness for "beautiful looking".

4.1   Types of Competitive Advantage

There are two ways a healthcare provider can develop a competitive advantage: One by Delivering a service at the lowest competitive cost compared to its rivals, meaning to say that pricing is the main competitive medium and two by Capturing and delivering a well differentiated service with unique attributes as discussed previously. According to Michael Porter, the pursuit of cost leadership mandates the finding and proper exploitation of all sources of cost advantage whereas differen-tiation is based on the provision of a valuable offering not just a low price [9, 10]. Both approaches low cost leadership and service differentiation have been discussed in the previous chapter, so the focus in this chapter will be on how different com-petitive advantages can be derived or extracted from these two strategies with a twist in their application in a hospital setting.

The first principle is *economy of scale* whereby an increase in the amount of units of sale results in a decrease in cost per unit [11]. The application of this principle is extremely important in business restructuring in any industry including healthcare. When an activity does not meet the required scale, either the volume should increase or the activity should be outsourced. There are many applications to this principle in hospital management and in particular in supply chain management where the use of economy of scale can help managers to reduce the cost of supply per unit. This can be achieved by Corralling the variability in usage of medical supplies by physicians, an initiative that mandates good physician engagement and integration. Narrowing the choices of supplies to a few will allow the purchaser to develop economy of scale and gain more bargaining power.

The second principle is *economy of learning*. The high repetitive rate of any activity has a beneficial effect both at the individual and organizational level. At the individual level economy of learning will result in improvement in dexterity and know how, and at the organizational level it will develop and refine routines where competencies are embedded [12]. A general surgeon who performs a large number of appendectomies will further refine his dexterity and technique with time thus reducing the operating room time and decreasing cost. Similarly at the organiza-tional level, Treating large volume of patients with the same condition will facilitate the development of management guidelines that can lead to establishment of clinical pathways that can help reduce the length of stay of patients, choice of medication and diagnostic tests, all of which leading to a reduced cost.

The third principle is *process re-engineering*. *Micheal Hammer* defined business process engineering as "–the fundamental rethinking and radical redesign of business processes to achieve dramatic improvements in critical contemporary measures of performance such as cost, quality, services and speed" [13]. This approach in redesigning operational processes is by large most applicable in healthcare nowadays where emphasis on patient's experience and satisfaction has become the center of patient care. An enhanced flow of patients and information thru process re-engineering can markedly improve patient care and satisfaction. More so process technology can help managers map job responsibilities across multifunctional tasks, identify bottle necks and constraints, recognize where problems reside and take decisions for improvement.

The fourth principle is *capacity utilization*. It is evident that an increase in utilization results in dilution of the fixed cost as the amount of expenditure per activity decreases [14]. This principle is commonly used in other industries where full capacity utilization reduces the fixed cost per unit of sale. In healthcare, utilization of the radiologic and laboratory facilities at maximum capacity results in marked reduction in the amount of fixed cost per test with subsequent decrease in the overall cost. Similarly Full utilization of the operating room results in marked spreading of the fixed cost such as salaries and utility fees over the number of surgeries, again leading to a decrease in the cost of procedures.

With respect to service differentiation, different types of competitive advantages can be derived. Service differentiation, as previously mentioned, is usually achieved when a healthcare provider delivers a service that is valuable to patients. In healthcare value is defined in terms of outcome, safety, quality of service delivered, and cost incurred. Outcome measures can be intermediate as in quality, utilization, efficiency, learning and accessibility, or final as in impact on quality of life and prevention of diseases [15]. Quality is defined by Webster as "—distinctive inherent feature" or "degree of excellence" [16]. In healthcare the definition of quality by the Institute of Medicine is "—The degree to which health services for individuals and populations increase the likelihood of desired health outcomes and are consistent with current professional knowledge" [17]. In both definitions Quality relates to distinctive features or attributes of a given service as perceived by the patient. Attributes of quality in medical service must be tangible such the high diagnostic yield of a given radiologic modality, short duration of stay, short recovery period after surgery, or the high rate of control of diabetes in an endocrinology clinic. Other forms of tangible attributes of quality are proxy measures of cleanliness or, the design and comfort of the waiting area.

Using differentiation as a strategy, a competitive advantage can also be derived by providing unique services of added value to patients. By looking within the institutional capabilities, the strategist must leverage on those of strategic relevance to create new drivers of uniqueness. Unique capabilities can be present in the efficiency of given processes, expertise of faculty and staff, and the seamless flow of patients. Other sources of competitive advantage include the breadth of procedures available such as bone marrow transplant in the oncology service, In Vitro-Fertilization in the Obstetric division, laser therapy for retinal detachment, treatment of intracranial aneurysm, or the use of robotic surgery. Differentiation can also occur through bundling of a medical service with complementary products. In healthcare this can be achieved by creating medical packages for patients, packages that include several touch points in the acquisition and consumption of a medical service. These can include transport to the medical center, lodging for family members, and provision of rehabilitation sessions following therapy.

In addition to the provision of unique services, competitive advantage can also derive from patient's needs after a thorough dissection of the different interfaces a patient comes across while seeking medical care. This dissection must go beyond the tangible attributes previously discussed to encompass non-tangible ones such as the social and psychological dimensions [18]. These can affect patient's access to medical information, the search process for medical facilities and the type of decision taking, be it heuristic or lexicographic given the constraints in resources.

In healthcare, the reputation and brand of a medical center and its faculty play a major role in differentiating it from its competitors. The psychological factor namely inspiring trust and confidence is essential to a successful differentiation. Similarly the social aspect plays an equal role in differentiating an institution from its competitors. A reputation to treat celebrities and the social network between patients and staff is a vital incentive for more referrals to that particular center.

4.2   Implementation and Sustainability of Value-Based Competition

After having discussed the different sources of competitive advantage, be it cost-leadership, service differentiation or both, it is empirical to develop and sustain value-based competition through the implementation of these strategies. As previously mentioned, value based competition is best built on the assumption of the "positive sum" competition where of all the stakeholders in healthcare from providers, employees, physicians, patients and family members are corners in sustaining a standardized optimal care.

Based on Porter Teisberg book on "Redefining Healthcare" there are eight principles to guide this transformation [19], three of which will be highlighted in this section. Principle one "Focus on Value, not just cost" emphasizes the importance of not trading service quality with cost, meaning to say the importance of providing both quality and low prices. Quality can have different perceptual evaluation based on the different perceiving sides and the various outcome measures used. From the healthcare provider's perspective it can be understood as the amount of dollars spent on a medical condition, whereas from the patient's perspective it can relate to functionality and quality of life after a procedure, extent of pain and emotional well-being. The second principle is "Competition is based on results". This latter, defined as "Actual health for patients" and not simply complying with processes and accreditation protocols, should be the driving principle for value-based competition. Competing on results will help in the development of not only "standardized practices" but will also promote "evidence based medicine", both of which will require physicians and healthcare providers to improve their methods of care, abide to standard approaches and compare themselves to best practices as a benchmark. The third principle focuses on the importance of centering value based competition over the full cycle of care. Both perspectives of quality in terms of Outcome relative to cost should be equally considered in value-based competition all along the cycle of care. This starts by setting the medical conditions deemed important, the myriad of services needed to address these conditions, and the beginning and end of the cycle of care encompassing the provision of these services. In the selection process of the medical condition, it is important to focus on conditions that benefit patients the most in the community at large. Likewise, in the selection of medical services the development of integrated practice units is crucial for management. In determining the start and end of the cycle of care several touch points must be considered such as environmental risk factors, genetic background, life style and last but not least the four steps in medical management, namely prevention, diagnosis, treatment and follow up. Developing value based competition in medical management that overlooks prevention and risk factors may not prevail. Within the medical management care practice, a low cost diagnosis followed by an expensive therapeutic intervention may defeat the purpose of a low cost strategy, and similarly a high diagnostic yield tempered by a low service therapy does not provide a value-based competition.

4.3   How to Sustain a Competitive Advantage

Competitive advantages are known to be self-eroded. Time and competition are the main factors contributing to the speed of that erosion. A competitor will start by identifying the main competitive advantage, diagnose its origin and once incentivized he will allocate the resources needed for imitation or innovating a new one. These diagnostic and imitative steps can be mitigated by either "obscuring the high performance" which is not recommended in healthcare, or by 'preemption" i.e., occupying potential strategic niches through patent proliferation or increasing the existing capacity [20].

References

1. Autry, P., and Thomas, D., 1986. Competitive Strategy in the Hospital Industry. *Health Care Management Review,* 11(no. 7), pp. 7–14.
2. Lamont, B.T., Marlin, D., and Hoffman, J.J., 1993. Porter's Generic Strategies, Porter s strategy low cost and differ.
3. Barney, J. (1991), 'Firm Resources and Sustained Competitive Advantage', *Journal of Management,* 17(1): 99–120.

4. Grant, R. M. (2013). *Contemporary Strategy Analysis, 8th Edition*, chapter 7 The sources and dimensions of competitive advantage, page 171–172.
5. Ghemawat, P. and Rivkin, JW. (2006), *Creating Competitive Advantage*, Harvard Business School note #9-798-062.
6. Stalk Jr, G. 1988 "Time: The next source of competitive advantage," Harvard Business Review (July/August, 1988);41–51.
7. Christensen, C.M., 2003. Six keys to building new markets by unleashing disruptive innovation.
8. Kim, W.C. and Mauborgne, R., 2004. Blue ocean strategy. *If you read nothing else on strategy, read thesebest-selling articles.* p. 71.
9. Porter, M.E., 1985. Competitive Advantage", New York: Free Press. *Porter Competitive Advantage 1985.*
10. Porter, M.E., 1985. Competitive Advantage", New York: Free Press. *Porter Competitive Advantage 1985.*
11. Grant, R. M. (2013). *Contemporary Strategy Analysis, 8th Edition*, chapter 7 The sources and dimensions of competitive advantage, page 180.
12. Argote, L., Beckman, S.L. and Epple, D., 1990. The persistence and transfer of learning in industrial settings. *Management science, 36*(2), pp. 140–154.
13. Hammer, M. and Champy, J., 1993. Reengineering the Corporation-a Manifesto for Business Revolution. New York 1994. *Davenport, TH: Process Innovation—Reengineering Work through Information Technology, Boston.*
14. Grant, R. M. (2013). *Contemporary Strategy Analysis, 8th Edition*, chapter 7 The sources and dimensions of competitive advantage, page 186.
15. Bradley, E. H., Pallas, S., Bashyal, C., Berman, P., Curry, L., 2010. Developing Strategies For Improving Health Care Delivery: Guide to Concepts, Determinants, Measurements, and Intervention Design. The World Bank 1818 H Street, NW.
16. Webster's Third New International Dictionary, Unabridged, Copyright 1993 Merriam-Webster, Incorporated.
17. Institute of Medicine, 2001. Crossing the Quality Chasm: A New Health System for the 21st Century. Washington, DC: National Academies Press.
18. Kotler, P., Keller, K.L., Koshy, A., 2012. A framework for marketing management, third edition, Chapter 5, *Analyzing Customer Markets*, pp. 84–87.
19. Porter, M.E. and Teisberg, E.O., 2006. *Redefining health care: creating value-based competition on results* chapter 4, page 98. Harvard Business Press.
20. Ma, H., 1999. Creation and preemption for competitive advantage. Management Decision, *37* (3), pp. 259–267.

Chapter 5
Innovation in Hospital Settings

In the second chapter of this book, the two main strategic views, positional and resource based were discussed with emphasis on the application of either in the context of environmental discontinuities and turbulence. Despite the added value of each approach in developing competitive advantages, more often than not firms are still competing fiercely to overcome the constantly increasing challenges. This has been attributed to the self-eroded nature of competitive advantages and the natural course of technology life cycle. The remain of competitive advantage can be pre-empted or masked by causal ambiguity, thus not allowing competitors to understand the basis of the product success [1]. Other means to sustain a competitive advantage is deterring entrants by having an aggressive reputation. Another cause for the increasingly challenging competitive arena is the self-limited life cycle of any technology that starts with experimentation, develop to maturity and ultimately phases out. Given these two constraints, namely the self-erosion of competitive advantages thru imitation and the disruptive end technology life-cycle, differentiation of existing attributes and defending one's market share are not enough to sustain competition. What is needed is innovation.

Innovation is invention that is commercialized [2]. Different sources of innovation have been described in the literature, most important of which are technology and market. Technology and or market knowledge are used to offer new products or services to an existing market, current or emerging one. Technological knowledge can be related to technological shifts in components, modules, linkages, and or processes, whereas market knowledge is often related to channels of distribution, application of new Marketing strategies or creation of New market segments or niches [3]. These latter are often referred to as streams of innovation. In a broad sense innovation could be defined as combination of producers and means of production, which includes new products, new methods of production, opening up new markets, and utilizing new raw materials.

In healthcare, technological shifts can materialize in the form of new drugs, new clinical guidelines and regimen, or the use of new surgical equipments and tools. This is seen with the introduction of new antibiotics, chemotherapeutic drugs and

© The Author(s) 2017
A. L. Hamdan, *Strategic Thinking in a Hospital Setting*,
SpringerBriefs in Public Health, DOI 10.1007/978-3-319-53597-5_5

the diverse application of robotic technology in surgery. Market knowledge on the other hand can also be very resourceful in healthcare innovation. Marketing information system can foster innovative approaches to patient care and advances in patient experience by providing feedback on what patients want. Social media has also created new marketing channels and platforms for communication with patients by providing information from the demand side, which is innovative in healthcare marketing.

Another equally important source of innovation is the organizational resources and competencies [4]. With the constraints in technological shifts and market information, firms more often than not lie on their own resources and capabilities to innovate. The innovation process starts by mapping the organization at three fronts, one the degree of innovation whether it is incrementally based on competence enhancement or discontinuous as based on radical shifts, two the locus of innovation whether innovation is architectural or component based, and last but not least for the extent or degree of bundling with the complementary assets [5]. In healthcare innovation is more often than not hybrid, with both incremental and radical innovation running in parallel. An example in general surgery is the enhancement in the type of sutures used for ligation and the introduction of hemostatic staplers (Endo Gia) in laparoscopic surgery in parallel.

Where does innovation stem from? Innovation occurs either across the firm's boundaries and platforms or within the firm. The micro-dynamics within the firm follows a value chain from Idea Generation to conversion of the idea into a product, and then to diffusion of the product across the organization. This in house creation followed by cross pollination, selection and development, is the natural course of innovation that leads to the spread of an innovative product or service within and across the institution and to the market place [6]. In health care this is often seen with the stemming of an innovative product or idea first within a division and then across the various departments. An example would be the development of a multidisciplinary program for the treatment of Head and Neck cancer or the development of a center of excellence for the management of sleep disorders. Cross pollination can also occur between different schools within an institution. An example would be the Development of 3-D imaging and printing of body organs to enhance the operative planning and surgical outcome. This project is the result of interdisciplinary collaboration between the school of engineering and faculty of medicine. This three Dimensional printing technique innovative idea has spread to involve the medical field in its application. What is equally important to the cross pollination and spreading of any invention is the ability to embed it in a business plan that takes into consideration the inherent risks and external threats. This process referred to as "Development" allows the creation of value out of the invention, which is a mandate for the transfer and adoption of the innovation by the market per say and the industry at large. The adoption of any new product or service is facilitated by the presence of an added value that allows the feasibility and success of its corresponding business plan. An example in laryngology would be the introduction of office based phonosurgical procedures for patients with voice disorders. These procedures carry different advantages that relate both to patient care and to cost. With respect to patient care, office based laryngology reduces the time of surgery, risk of general anesthesia and post-operative recovery. Similarly, these procedures carry financial benefits by reducing the overall cost and expenses incurred in the course of the treatment. This latter is a major added value that increases the financial feasibility of a business plan that aims at updating the equipment in a laryngology practice.

Despite the aforementioned examples of sources of innovation in healthcare, this latter has been discretionary if not discouraged in the healthcare industry. This negative and conservative approach has been attributed to the limited short term effects of innovation on results of medical care, and to the natural resistance of staff and physicians to any change in the cycle of care of patients [7]. Though investment in health care innovation has been somewhat rewarding with a return of $2–$3 dollars for every dollar invested, it has met a lot of skepticism, mostly due to the constant rise in health care expenditure despite the advances attributed to innovation. This can be partially explained based on the fact that innovation has been restricted to the medical treatment of few chronic conditions such as cancer, stroke and cardiac disease and has missed many other conditions [8]. Another obstacle to innovation is the "lack of competition on results" [9], meaning to say that innovation per say is not enough to make a change when the problem lies in the adoption and implementation of the innovative ideas by physicians in their medical practice. Hence innovation must be enabled by results, results that show the added value of adopting the innovative idea in the care of patients. Other causes why innovation is discouraged aside from the resistant mindset of medical practitioners and the skewing of practice guidelines by drug companies are lack of accountability and reimbursement practices in health care [10].

Despite all the obstacles to innovation, different forms of innovation in healthcare management have been described. Based on Porter Teisburg book on "Redefining Healthcare" [7], innovation can be in a "new facility, new organizational structure, new processes, or new form of collaboration across providers". With these forms are numerous applications to Innovation in health care. It can assist in fostering value-based competition by either improving short-term results in the management of chronic diseases, or by shortening the cycle of care. Example of short term result is the introduction of new antibiotic that shortens the days of sickness and improves patient's compliance, or the introduction of a new thrombolytic agent that reduces the stay of patients in the intensive care unit and hence decreases cost. Example of how innovation can shorten the cycle of care is the introduction of minimally invasive surgery. This latter has changed the whole cycle of care by reducing the length of stay, morbidity of surgery and the post-operative care.

5.1 How to Prepare an Organization for Innovation

Any organization is subject to incremental change in thriving to maintain or grow its market share. Nevertheless, given the universal aspect of the technological life cycle, namely the ferment era characterized by experimentation and entrepreneurship, the dominant era where consensus has been reached in terms of product or service attributes, and the incremental phase distinctive by variations on these attributes, a radical innovation is needed to sustain growth and productivity [11]. This radical move invariably stems from a disruptive technology that punctuates a rather seamlessly steady incremental innovation. This latter unless interrupted by a discontinuity that creates a sense of urgency for a radical change, incremental innovation will only result in improvement in the performance or attributes of the product at hand, which more often than not, is not enough to allow the leap needed for an institution to survive. Two interesting examples in healthcare ought to be mentioned in this context: One is the hearing aid transition from a post-auricular device to a trans-canal one, accounting not only for the quality of sound but also for the cosmetic and functionality of using hearing aids. Two is the radical shift from open abdominal surgery to laparoscopic surgery, though both lead to the same result in terms of surgical outcome, the latter carries less morbidity, shorter duration of stay, and faster recovery.

To that end, institutions at large need to be ready and equipped to undergo both incremental and radical innovation in order to survive competition and sustain growth. Below are four tactics that can be adopted in order to prepare an institution for innovation.

5.1.1 Developing Organizational Ambidexterity

By definition, Ambidexterity is the ability to use both hands equally, having the versatility and agility to duplicate with both hands [12]. An organization is said to have ambidexterity if it can manage short term efficiency by emphasizing stability and control and can manage long term innovation by taking risks and learning by doing [13]. In other words, an organization should be equipped to manage incremental change using conventional managerial wisdom based on centralization and pursuit of well-engineered processes, and radical innovation by taking risks, adopting a decentralized approach with the establishment of small functional units.

> In a hospital setting, incremental innovation is maintained thru quality management control, use of balanced score cards, and the feedback from patient experience surveys, whereas radical innovation can be pursued thru the establishment of cross functional teams that encourage innovative ideas and value experimentation.

Members of the team can be any stakeholder in healthcare, from physicians, nursing staff to biomedical engineers and medical students.

5.1.2 Increasing the Ratio of Exploration to Exploitation

Exploitation is using the current resources and capabilities of the institution to increase productivity and efficiency. In other words, exploitation increases the output given the same input. Exploration is reconfiguring the existing resources and capabilities in order not just to meet the obvious goals but to take risks and venture in reaching the stretch ones [14]. An example in health care would be the allocation of grants for research proposal, the result of which may not always bear significant added value in clinical practice on the short term. Despite the questionable return and the inherent risks, yet resources are often allocated for a given investigation, keeping in mind its long term implications.

5.1.3 Knowledge Brokering

This third tactic is the most valuable if we were to consider innovation as rebirth or re-incarnation of old ideas in new forms and shapes. Many innovators believe that innovation is about spotting old ideas, be it forms, material or design, and implementing these in a new context, thus bringing new value to old concepts, values that are commensurate with the current needs and demands of the market [15]. It is the art of scouting by assuming the right vantage position and applying the right skills to frame your catch in the right context. Based on Andrew Hargadon and Robert I. Sutton [16], knowledge brokering cycle consists of four intertwined acts: One is Capturing old ideas by scanning different firms and industries looking for old ideas and concepts. Thomas Edisson said that "To invent you need imagination and a pile of Junk" [17]. Two is keeping these ideas alive. Cognitive psychologists believe that the major cause of not finding a solution is not ignorance but inability of individuals to put their finger on the necessary information at the right point in time. This can be done by keeping notes, power points and by having the rapid response team. Three is imagining new uses for the old ideas, find new domains of application. Four is by putting promising concepts to test: A good idea for a new product is not worth much itself, if not tested and turned into a sellable item.

5.1.4 Network and Filling Structural Hole

Network analysis provides a map that identifies the role and position of all the economic players in the market and the ties through which information flows. Networks affect markets by carrying information, by creating means to harvest and recombine resources, and by generating new opportunities. Netting can also feed into a virtuous cycle whereby the increase in network size leads to an increase in the adoption of users which in turn leads to an increase in reputation, all of which leads to economy of scale [18]. The applications of Netting in health care are over-whelming and cannot be overemphasized. A hospital business lies primarily on its network with its patient base, community alliances, referring physicians, and neighbouring medical practitioners.

On the other hand, a gap in the network where ties do not exist is often referred to as structural hole. Filling this structural hole is beneficial as it allows managers to assume new roles and add value to the market. The challenge is to increase unit dependence, manage network resilience, identify new linkages, and convert weak ties into resource routines. In a hospital setting, a structural hole can lie in the discontinuity of a referral channel, or lack of acknowledgment of a key player in the referring network. Filling this structural hole can be achieved by building a new strategic alliance with either a neighboring hospital, group of physicians or third party payers, all of which leads to improvement in practice, more referrals and higher revenue.

5.2 Enablers for Innovation

As previously mentioned innovation if not well adopted and implemented, cannot bring new value to the institution. Various means for enabling innovation can be used and these are listed below:

a. First and foremost is the Change in mindset at the individual level. There has to be a paradigm shift in thinking from the causal reasoning which is focused on predictive goals and outcomes to effectual reasoning which is more flexible and afford possible losses by leveraging on contingencies. This change in cognitive frame allows daring actions such as rejection of pre-existing beliefs and building of new partnerships, thus creating a more receptive platform for Inventions and innovation [19]. In a hospital setting, this mind-shift starts at the level of chairpersons, head of divisions and administrators. Though medical errors need to be avoided and there is little room for morbidities in medical practice, leaders must nourish the open-mindedness and welcome new thoughts that foster Patient centered care and team work. An example would be the introduction of a new process for flow of patients in the operating room that would reduce the waiting time, devising a new oral airway that delivers oxygen and provides suction simultaneously [20], or a new surgical approach in injection laryngo-plasty [21].

b. Second you need to examine the ecosystem, which allows either the success or failure of an innovative product. It is this collaborative arrangement between the different firms that contribute to the offering of a customer solution through the provision of innovation [22]. The ecosystem accentuates the importance of all firms in the creation of value and defines the landscape for the development, transfer and consolidation of inventions, taking into account the risk of initia-tion, the risk of interdependence and that of integration. In other words, innovators must allocate the right resources to mitigate any risk at the start, chose the right collaborators for interdependence and last but not least ascertain proper adoption of the innovative product. Two examples in the medical field are illustrated: One is the introduction of a medical service that is still very embryonic and has poor public awareness such as stem cell therapy. Despite the large amount of resources allocated for this innovative treatment modality, regenerative medicine is still frowned upon by most practitioners. Another example is the introduction of new technology that is not well accommodated for in the operating room, such as the use of robotic surgery.

> A given space, a well-trained team and an information system are needed to benefit the most from this technological advancement.

c. Third is proper understanding of the Complementary products and appropriability: In order to develop and sustain core value innovation you need to examine the status of the complementary assets whether these are freely available or held tightly and the imitability of your value innovation. That being said, your design will dominate or not depends on your complementary assets and the appropriability of your product. In other words you need to bundle with complementary assets [23]. A good example is the introduction of clinical pathways in medical practice. Clinical pathways have been advocated as a means to standardize care of patients and to provide benchmarks in medical practice. Another equally important added value is the control of expenditure in healthcare and the order of unnecessary tests. The success of clinical pathways is strongly contingent on the presence of electronic medical record in order to limit and alert physicians when an order for a prescription is made.

References

1. Porter, M. E. (2011). Competitive advantage of nations: creating and sustaining superior performance. Simon and Schuster.
2. Grant, R. M. (2013). Contemporary Strategy Analysis, 8th Edition, chapter 7 The sources and dimensions of competitive advantage, page 247
3. Afuah, A. (2003), 'Models of Innovation', chapter 2 in Innovation Management: Strategies, Implementation and Profits, Oxford: Oxford University Press.
4. Barney, J. (1991), 'Firm Resources and Sustained Competitive Advantage', Journal of Management, 17(1): 99–120.
5. Victor P Seidel, Lecture Title: Innovation Intensity, given in Diploma in Strategy and Innovation Oxford University, April 2014.
6. Grant, R. M. (2013). Contemporary Strategy Analysis, 8th Edition, chapter 7 The sources and dimensions of competitive advantage, page 247–8

7. Porter, M.E. and Teisberg, E.O., 2006. Redefining health care: creating value-based competition on results. Harvard Business Press, chapter 4, page 140.
8. MEDTAP Intenational, 2004. Inc. The value of Invetsment in Health Care: Bettre care, Bettre lives. Bethesda, MD; MEDTAP International. http://www.medtap.com/Products/HP-FullReport.pdf
9. Porter, M.E. and Teisberg, E.O., 2006. Redefining health care: creating value-based competition on results. Harvard Business Press, chapter 4, page 143
10. Porter, M.E. and Teisberg, E.O., 2006. Redefining health care: creating value-based competition on results. Harvard Business Press, chapter 4, page 145
11. Bower, J.L. and Christensen, C.M., 1995. Disruptive technologies: catching the wave (pp. 506–20). Harvard Business Review.
12. Merriam Webster Dictionary 1928
13. O'Reilly, CA. III and Tushman. ML. (2011), 'Organizational Ambidexterity in Action: How Managers Explore and Exploit', California Management Review, 53(4): 1–18.
14. Nimgade, A. (2007), IDEO Product Development, Harvard Business School case #9-600-143.
15. Hargadon, A., & Sutton, R. I. (1999). Building an innovation factory. Harvard business review, 78(3), 157–66.
16. Hargadon, A. and Sutton, RI. (2000), 'Building an innovation factory', Harvard Business Review, 78(3): 157–166.
17. Dong, A., 2011. The role of affect in creative minds. In New perspectives on affect and learning technologies (pp. 217–232). Springer New York.
18. Nichols-Casebolt, A., Figueira-McDonough, J. and Netting, F.E., 2000. Change strategies for integrating women's knowledge into social work curricula. Journal of Social Work Education, 36(1), pp. 65–78.
19. Sarasvathy, S.D., 2001, August. Effectual reasoning in entrepreneurial decision making: existence and bounds. In Academy of management proceedings (Vol. 2001, No. 1, pp. D1–D6). Academy of Management.
20. Soweid, A.M., Yaghi, S.R., Jamali, F.R., Kobeissy, A.A., Mallat, M.E., Hussein, R. and Ayoub, C.M., 2011. Posterior lingual lidocaine: no el et od to i ro e no el et od to i ro e no el et od to i ro e tolerance in u er gastrointestinal endosco y. endoscopy, 17(47), pp. 5191–5196.
21. Hamdan, A.L., Ziade, G., Jaffal, H. and Skaff, G., 2015. Transnasal Injection Laryngoplasty. Annals of Otology, Rhinology & Laryngology
22. Adner, R. (2006), 'Match Your Innovation Strategy to Your Innovation Ecosystem', Harvard Business Review, 84(4): 98–107.
23. Rothaermel, F.T., 2001. Incumbent's advantage through exploiting complementary assets via interfirm cooperation. Strategic Management Journal, 22(6–7), pp. 687–699.

Chapter 6
Strategic Framework in a Hospital Settings

In the development of a strategic framework, it is important to keep note of the Industry economics and drivers of change. The main drivers of change in health care are many and include demographic changes, social and lifestyle changes, explosion in medical knowledge, advances in technology as well as the increase in public awareness regarding the early need to seek medical attention. To this end, in order to achieve a sound strategic framework, it is important to perform proper external and internal environment analysis, summary of the competitive dynamics followed by selection of the right strategic variables that help the strategist reach the desired goals and objectives.

6.1 External Environmental Analysis

The external environment can be analyzed using different diagnostic tools that help the strategist obtain a 360° view of the competitive arena in the healthcare industry. Among these are the PESTEL analysis, the competitive five forces, industry maturity, industry key success factors, and threats and opportunities.

6.1.1 PESTEL

We will start by analyzing six important denominators present in any business environment often referred to as PESTEL [1]. The healthcare political plan controls the provision or lack of provision of resources, which ultimately impacts the practice of healthcare providers and their ability to cater for patients' needs. Similarly the social and economic conditions cannot stay afloat of the healthcare expenses and spending. The economic growth or regression underpins the short and long term prosperity of the medical sector, be it tertiary or primary, with marked

© The Author(s) 2017
A. L. Hamdan, *Strategic Thinking in a Hospital Setting*,
SpringerBriefs in Public Health, DOI 10.1007/978-3-319-53597-5_6

impact on practitioners and patients. The technological innovations, pervasiveness and rate of diffusion have also an impact on the health care sector. The recent advances in medical science witnessed by various leaders in different specialties, have shaped the practice in many institutions and led to shifts in the current guidelines and the development of new protocols. Environmental factors such as pollution and gas emission have also influenced medical care by either accentuating certain medical conditions or by altering the progress of others. Last but not least are the legal and regulatory constraints that may deter the introduction of new therapeutic modes or mitigate the implementation of innovative approaches.

In parallel with PESTEL analysis strategist often perform customer analysis. This latter includes Market segmentation and niche thorough examination of patient's needs, visit patterns and price sensitivity [2]. It is important to note that niche marketing must be factored in relation to patient's individual needs and physician's style of practice. The segmentation may be based on demographic variables, socio-economic or health related issues taking into consideration the discretionary offerings of individual services often referred to by Anderson and Narus as the "Flexible market Offering" [3]. Health care managers must incorporate in their marketing strategy the different market segments in attempt to match the needs of those segments with the core competencies and capabilities of their corresponding institution. Proper matching is crucial for the success of any medical service and for patient's satisfaction. This latter can be gauged by the visit patterns and loyalty which are also affected by price sensitivity and nature of the payer mix.

6.1.2 Competitive Forces

In parallel with the customer analysis, a strategist must examine the competitive forces of the market and integrate these in a constructive manner. These forces not only drive competition but also determine the profitability of the medical institution within the health care sector. It is crucial to understand these forces if we were to foresee the market position of healthcare providers. The five forces that shape Industry competition as reported by Porter are: "Threat of new entrants", "bargaining power of suppliers", "bargaining power of Buyers", "Threat of substitute products or services", and "Rivalry among existing competitors" [4].

6.1.2.1 Threat of Entry

The emergence of new entrants within an industry exerts pressure on price and cost. The behaviour of the incumbents varies with the severity of the threat leading either to lower the prices or to a radical change in strategy [5]. In a hospital setting, a large capacity managed efficiently with high utilization rate can mitigate threats of entry by improving the "supply-side economy of scale" [5]. Other forms of barriers to entry include word of mouth which perpetuates referrals to a given physician or institution, and a high switching cost for a patient which puts new entrants at a disadvantage. A witness to this barrier is the design of a healthcare system whereby polyclinics or hospitals drain a given geographic area [6]. In health care barriers to new entrants can be circumvented by staying at the forefront in diagnostic and therapeutic technological advances, by sustaining and enriching the hospital network with its strategic allies, and last but not least by fostering research be it clinical or basic.

6.1.2.2 Power of Suppliers

In a hospital setting, there is a large diversity in the power of suppliers. Some may be dominant as in the case of an exclusive supplier of a well differentiated medical supply, or when the supplier sponsors medical activities and training of physicians. The provision of a well differentiated service compounded with a high switching cost for the hospitals empowers markedly the supplier, more so of he/she has the capacity to further integrate in the healthcare industry [6].

6.1.2.3 Power of Buyers

A hospital that does not provide a well differentiated service, one with an added value is more likely to lose its patient base with time, whereas investing in sub-specialized services will help create a niche market that is hard to imitate. The more sub-specialized a medical center is, the more differentiated the services become, thus weakening the bargaining power of patients. On the other hand, hospital managers and strategies should remain on the watch out for the "too demanding customers" as these can markedly drive up the cost [7].

6.1.2.4 The Threat of Substitutes

In the health care industry, the threats of substitutes are few given the uniformity and clinical guidelines in medical practice. Nevertheless, when present these can be mitigated by having good patient loyalty programs and by maintaining a healthy patient- physician relationship [5–7].

6.1.2.5 Rivalry Among Existing Competitors

This can manifest itself as price discounting, introduction of new products, advertising campaigns and service improvements. The degree to which rivalry drives down an industry's potential profit depends on the intensity with which companies compete and the basis on which they compete. The **intensity** of rivalry is amplified when competitors are numerous, the industry growth is slow, the exit barriers are high or when the rivals are highly **committed** to the business and have goals beyond economic performance [5, 6]. Rivalry becomes destructive when it gravitates solely to price, which is mostly vulnerable when the fixed cost is high, and the product is perishable. That is why it is crucial to price the services taking into consideration the value offered as well as the customer's will to pay [8].

In the health care sector, rivalry is markedly affected by the commitment of healthcare providers to their patients and community at large, and their ability to meet patient's need at an affordable cost. When present, rivalry can exist in various ways such as with the establishment of centers of excellence that focus on specific disease entities, where the focus is on the way the service is being rendered, the post-discharge patient care, or by incorporating other features from different industries into the medical field, such as accommodation service to the patient himself/herself and family members. It is not uncommon nowadays to see medical centers incorporating attributes of luxurious hotel to better accommodate their patient's needs. No doubt, this hybrid service, medical and lodging, entails a major strategic thinking and structural changes within the medical sector; Last but not least, a competitive advantage may be derived by specializing in one particular domain, reducing the heterogeneity of services and focusing on specific medical products and procedures.

6.1.3 Industry Maturity

Industry maturity reflects the potential growth of a given industry given the constant demographic changes and the perpetual increase in patients' needs. It is a summary statement of the stability, predictability and growth potential of the industry and or its corresponding segments. As such it defines the competitive, financial and management dynamics of that industry. Four basic stages are usually described; Embryonic, Growth, Mature, and Aging, with each stage having distinct characteristics that are based mainly on the aforementioned competitive forces [9]. Normally an industry moves through these four basic stages or can remain in one stage over a long period of time.

In the healthcare industry, the need for medical services is invariably in constant growth given the demographic changes and the increase in demand for healthcare facilities. Other causes for this growth are the increase in public awareness and the ease of accessibility to medical services [10, 11]. Nevertheless, despite this steady increase for the need to seek medical care across all specialties, there are differences in maturity across the various sub-specialties. For instance the audiology service might be in the maturity phase whereas robotic surgery and use of navigation devices during surgery are still growing. The proper matching of a given specialty to the corresponding phase of the industry maturity bears important sequelae especially regarding allocation of resources. A maturing product in a given industry may be less appealing for investment compared to a growing product.

6.1.4 Key Success Factors in the Healthcare Industry

The client or patient's purchasing criteria for a medical service ought to be matched to the industry key success factors in order for the act of purchasing to take place. There are many key success factors in medical practice and healthcare provision, some integral to the competencies of the service provided and others linked to proxy measures such accessibility, cleanliness of the premises and flow of patients [12, 13]. Below is a short list:

1. Geographic location
2. Accessibility to premises and services
3. Delivery of services in terms of quality and performance
4. Provision of up to date technology
5. Date and time of appointment
6. Waiting time
7. Greeting of staff
8. Logistics in paper work
9. Financial coverage and pay logistics
10. Cost of service
11. Value for money
12. Time spent with physician
13. Impersonality of physician
14. Competence of physician
15. Adequacy of follow up.

Most important of all these key success factors is the ability to serve the patient thru customization. Despite the presence of limited number of diseases and the use of well-defined diagnostic and therapeutic guidelines, physicians are often challenged to meet the needs of patients as individuals. What we are alluding to is the need to individualize medical care to match the diversity in the clinical presentation. This diversity in clinical presentation mandates different approaches and hence more individual care. This leads us to say that there is an emerging and growing need to customize medical service despite the commonality in clinical presentation.

6.1.5 Threat of Opportunities

There are numerous threats to one's practice. These can include the emergence of a new competitor, new policies of reimbursement with third party payers, new governmental healthcare rules and regulations, loss of strategic alliances, change in payer mix, economic crisis, political instability and many others. A sound strategic plan may be able to convert some of the adversities and threats into opportunities by re-assessing the potential sequel of each in a different context.

Opportunities in medical practice and healthcare in general may be exemplified by the emergence of a new technology, a new product, innovative service or by shifts in demographic changes. Opportunities may also rise with loss of a competitor or lack of a dominant one, by the surge of a new market segment that has been vacated, by vertical or horizontal integration, or by low barrier to entering a new market [14].

6.2   Internal Environment Analysis

There are many elements to analyze in the internal environment, starting with strength and weaknesses of a given institution, its inherent capabilities and competencies, its usage of resources for efficiency, its utilization rate, performance and quality, to the level of its offering vis-à-vis the key success factors in the industry of healthcare. Another key component for internal environment analysis is the culture of the working environment, which is critical to the success of multidisciplinary care.

6.2.1   Strength and Weaknesses

It is important to note that strength and weaknesses may override one another pending on the context of performance. Strength at one point in time may become a weakness and vice versa a weakness may become strength [15]. An example would be the reputation of an institution. This latter can be a core strength in reputing one's image and soliciting referrals, however once injured or damaged it becomes a major weakness. Similarly tacit information is a strength however if not well processed and recorded it may erode and thus weakens the knowledge base of the institution. Other examples of strength and weakness are listed below.

6.2.1.1   Strength

1. A new service
2. A capability
3. A core competency
4. Brand and reputation
5. Special expertise
6. Accessibility
7. Low cost

8. Efficiency and high rate of utilization
9. High performance
10. High patient satisfaction score
11. Good patient experience.

6.2.1.2 Weaknesses

1. Lack of technology
2. Understaff
3. Lack of given expertise\Lack of transparency
4. Lack of administrative support
5. Organizational structure and centralization
6. Poor differentiation of services.

6.2.2 Capabilities and Competencies

Capabilities by definition are the productive assets of the firm, i.e. the outcome of its resources. These can be tangible such as concrete assets and cash flow or intangible such as a brand image or well-engineered processes [16]. When properly deployed, resources and capabilities assist in the production of an end-product or service along the value chain. In a hospital setting, capabilities can reside in the efficiency of hospital admission processes, length of patient's stay, yield of its radiologic services or the capacity of its operating room. Capabilities can also reside in quality measures among which are the clinical and managerial qualities. The clinical quality is measured by the extent of adherence to evidence based medicine and well established guidelines and protocol, whereas the managerial quality is measured by the use of balanced scorecards, availability of supplies and equipment and the use of functional records. Other measures of quality include patient experience which is the final outcome measure of patient centered care [17]. Capabilities can also reside in the extent to which an institution allocates human resources in patient care. The extent of engagement can be gagged by looking at the staff to patient ratio and degree of integration of staff in patient management. Other Examples of capabilities and competencies are the areas of expertise of its faculty, the training and development of staff, the provision of unique services, branding and so forth.

When capabilities are of strategic relevance, these are labeled as competencies. Common examples of competencies are excellence in patient care, organizational design and Information system such as data-warehousing. Excellence in clinical care is a major competence that needs to be cultivated with the main approach being "patient centered approach" [18].

In parallel, high priority is often given to the issue of organizational design because this later presents not only the micro structure of the organization but also its various subcomponents [19]. Appropriate organization structure is key to the success of the strategic plan of any organization confronted with the various threats of the external environment and the internally growing conflicts. In parallel with the turbulent needs of the healthcare environment is the increased divergence in the demands of the market. This has led medical institutions to convert from a mechanistic model characterized by rigidity, bureaucracy to a dynamic constantly adapting organic model. Instead of a command-and-control system, a rather collaborative system is being developed and implemented.

Another important capability that can be of major strategic relevance is culture. Culture is defined as the sum of properties common to a group to which consensus has been made. It is the product of internal as well as external integration processes between the organization itself on one end and the micro and macro-environment on the other end [20]. The adaptation to the daily interactions processes and conflicts result in a common understanding of what is the basic culture of the organization. That consensus is more often than not, a major competence that ought to be examined in the internal environment analysis of any strategic plan.

Other important dimensions that need to be measured in the Internal Environment Analysis are measures of performance. These include the level of performance of the institution vis-à-vis the key success factors, measures of efficiency and utilization, measures of human resources engagement, in addition to measures of quality, accessibility, learning and sustainability [17]. In measuring the level of performance of the institution vis-à-vis the key success factors of the industry, the strategist often needs to answer questions such as: Where do we stand in terms of patient's experience and satisfaction? How accessible are we both geographically and financially? How is the diagnostic yield of the institution compared to the market? How is the waiting time? Is the staff competent enough? Do we offer state of the art technology?

Equally important measures and dimensions of performance are efficiency and utilization. Measures for efficiency can include cost-to-service ratio, staff to service ratio, and patient and volume procedure in relation to capacity and number of physicians, whereas measures of utilization include patient volume and physician number in relation to capacity [21, 22]. It is also important to examine the extent and level of performance of the human resources within the institution. Questions such as what is the extent of staff engagement? How far is the support of the administration? And to what extent are the physicians a source of referral?

Summary of Competitive Dynamics
In summary, after having performed an external and an internal environment analysis, a summary of the competitive dynamics will define the industry attractiveness, namely healthcare, and the competitive or strategic position of the medical institution.

The Industry attractiveness is a function of both, competitive intensity and Industry maturity [23]. *A highly competitive and mature industry is less likely to be attractive than a low competitive and embryonic one. That same interplay between industry maturity and competitive intensity can be used to assess the attractiveness of medical services within an institution and their corresponding markets. Robotic surgery for instance is an attractive product strategically because it is still in its embryonic or growing phase and is not highly competitive whereas laparoscopic surgery is less attractive given the fact that it is highly competitive and is readily available in many medical institutions. It is important to note that though a product or service may not be strategically attractive yet it can be very lucrative as is the case of a cash cow product in many industries.*

1. The degree to which a market or a service is attractive or not carries two important implications: One is the window of opportunity associated with the attractiveness. A highly attractive service is appealing strategically because it opens a window of opportunity and a source of competitive advantage especially if well invested in. A hospital may distinguish itself by providing an attractive and hard to imitate service, which in turn can act as a strong leverage to gain more market share and expand. The other important implication of service attractiveness is resource allocation. This latter depends not only on the opportunities for profit but also on the capabilities and perspectives a company have in order to capture these opportunities. In the health care industry, a hospital that has an open eye for emerging opportunities must also have the right perspective and adequate resources to invest in these opportunities. As such, market or service attractiveness is not enough to develop a competitive advantage, a proper vision, compiled with an adequate strategic and financial plan is needed to capture a growing opportunity [24]. For instance a voice unit in a city rich in entertainment events will assume a leadership/strong position that will be sustained throughout the maturation of the industry of vocal care because of its early entry into the market and the competitive advantages previously mentioned.

Strategic position is usually mapped on a matrix with the competitive position and industry growth along its two axes. The competitive position of any institution is based on its core competences reflected by its market share and its level of offering vis-à-vis the key success factors [25]. The importance of this later may vary according to the industry maturity and growth as shown in the competitive intensity section. In order to sustain and increase their market share, hospitals and medical institutions have to remain at the forefront in differentiating their services while keeping a competitive cost. Early market entry and sustaining advances in technology allow hospitals to keep a competitive advantage and sustain their market share despite the possible surging of new competitors in this field. This means they will be capable of maintaining their long term position with little effect of the actions taken by its competitors. Thus its strategic position will not endanger their long term direction and market share.

References

1. Mamouny, A. and Hanoune, M., Enterprise ontology utilization for information retrieval in competitive intelligence process.
2. Dalgic, T. and Leeuw, M., 1994. Niche marketing revisited: concept, applications and some European cases. *European Journal of Marketing, 28*(4), pp. 39–55.
3. Anderson, J.C. and Narus, J.A., 1995. Capturing the value of supplementary services. *Harvard Business Review, 73*(1), pp. 75–83.
4. M.E.Porter, 2008 "The five competitive Forces that shape Strategy," Harvard Business Review 57 (January 2008): 57–71.
5. Porter.M.E., Olmsted Teisberg.E, PhD. 2007. *How Physicians Can Change the Future of Health Care.* JAMA, 297, pp. 1103–1111.
6. Porter,M. E., 1998. Competitive Strategy: Techniques for Analyzing Industries and Competitors. Simon and Schuster.
7. Wolf, J.A. 2013. The patient experience: strategies and approaches for providers to achieve and maintain a competitive advantage. Bedford, TX: The Beryl Institute.
8. Menduno, M., 2001. Priced to perfection. *Business,* 2, pp. 40–42.
9. Levitt, T., 1965. "Exploit The Product Life Cycle", *Harvard Business Review.*
10. United Nations Population Division, World Population Prospects, 2008.
11. Vipperla, R., Renals, S. and Frankel, J., 2010. Ageing voices: The effect of changes in voice parameters on ASR performance. *EURASIP Journal on Audio, Speech, and Music Processing, 2010*(1), p. 1.
12. Hofer, C.W. and Schendel, D., 1980. *Strategy formulation: Analytical concepts.* West Publishing.
13. Jeffery, R., 2009. Key Success Factors for Private Hospital Medical Group, *Group Practice Journal,* Volume 58, No 5.
14. Kotler, P., Keller, K.L., 2007.A framework For Marketing Management, Third Edition,, Chapter 2,Developing and Implementing Marketing Strategies Plan, p. 30.
15. Law, J., 2010. *A dictionary of accounting.* Oxford University Press.
16. Barney, J., 1991. Firm resources and sustained competitive advantage.*Journal of management, 17*(1), pp. 99–120.
17. Donabedian, A., 1980. *The Definition of Quality and Approaches to Its Assessment.* Ann Arbor, MI: Health Administration Press.
18. Robison J., 2010. What is the "patient experience?" *Gallup Management Journal* [Online]. Available at: http://businessjournal.gallup.com/content/143258/patient-experience.aspx. 2010. [Accessed March 15, 2014].
19. Daft, R.L., 2004. *Organization Theory and Design,* 8th ed.
20. O'Reilly, C.A., Chatman, J. and Caldwell, D.F., 1991. People and organizational culture: A profile comparison approach to assessing person-organization fit. *Academy of management journal, 34*(3), pp. 487–516.
21. Hollingsworth, B. 2008. "The measurement of Efficiency and Productivity of Health Care Delivery". *Health Economics.* 17:1107–28.
22. Green L. and V. Nguyen 2001. "Strategies for cutting Hospital Beds: The Impact on Patient Service." *Health Services Research.* 36(2):421–42.
23. Jeffrey F.Rayport and Bernard J.Jaworsku, *E-Commerce* (New York: McGraw-Hill, 2001), p. 53.
24. Mahoney, J.T. and Pandian, J.R., 1992. The resource-based view within the conversation of strategic management. *Strategic management journal, 13*(5), pp. 363–380.
25. Prahalad, C.K. and Hamel, G., 1990. "The Core Competence of the Corporation". *Harvard Business Review,* pp. 79–91.

Chapter 7
Eight Strategic Tools Implemented

Strategies to Reduce Cost, Increase Load and Revenue

Given the financial constraints in healthcare, most managers are challenged to meet common goals pertaining cost, revenue and quality. Among others these include, improvement in patient experience, improvement in operational performance, improvement in administrative support and organizational structure, sustained and increased medical expertise, while reducing cost and increasing the load. These can be achieved using both differentiation strategy and low cost leadership in parallel with global netting for widening the breadth of strategic alliances and partnership.

In this section eight strategies to reduce cost, increase load and revenue will be described. These strategies stem from five strategic directions geared towards meeting the aforementioned goals and servicing the different stakeholders of the concerned institution and the community at large. One is evolution in patient care, two is integration between patient care and research, three is coherence and alignment in competencies, four is financial viability and sustainability, and five is gaining global netting.

The main strategic projects to reduce cost, increase revenue, differentiate quality of care and improve operational efficiency that will be discussed in this chapter are:

The "S2P—project", The "Group purchasing project", The "Nero-project", The "Clinical pathway project", The "Patient Loyalty Program", The "Physician Liaison program", The "Physician Integration program", and The "Staff engagement program".

For each of these projects there will be operational initiatives, strategic indicators, description of current state or position when present and the three year target.

© The Author(s) 2017
A. L. Hamdan, *Strategic Thinking in a Hospital Setting*,
SpringerBriefs in Public Health, DOI 10.1007/978-3-319-53597-5_7

7.1   The "S2P Project"

Traditionally value creation has been heavily based on value chain analysis with the focus being on cost reduction and or value creation. Along this conceptual model, cost leadership and value creation are delivered either upstream as input or downstream as output. A rather innovative approach would focus on reconfiguring the role of the players in the delivery of healthcare with patient's interest being at the center. This will be the basis of the S2P project where S stands for Surgeon and Supplier and P for purchasing.

As in any game, creating value starts by identifying the key elements namely the players, the added value of each, the rules and their tactics, in addition to the scope of the game. In the S2P project the key players are the surgeons assuming the role of the consumers, the suppliers providing the supplies and medicals tools consumed by the surgeons, and the purchasing department which represents the institution's interest. Each of the players has an added value that will be reconfigured in the S2P project in order to create better alliances and improve outcome for all. The rules defined conventionally by the role of each player will be tailored differently allowing more input and intervention from each with the purpose of reducing cost and improving value. The scope lies within the realm of patient's interest and care. This is illustrated in Fig. 7.1.

7.1.1   Facets of the S2P Project

The S2P has two facets to it.

Fig. 7.1 Triad of S2P

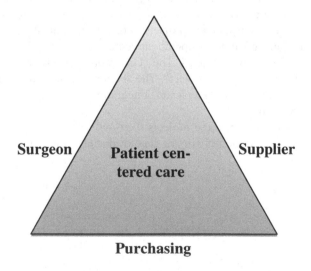

Surgeon   **Patient centered care**   Supplier

Purchasing

7.1.1.1 Value Constellation [1]

This is achieved by allowing physicians to reduce cost and add value to the supplies used in the operating room. In the first phase of this project, physicians' engagement will allow improvement in the contribution margin and in the second phase it will allow value creation.

> Supplies will be tailored in a way to reduce the purchasing cost without compromising the supplies' quality of material or the scope of their usage.

7.1.1.2 Emphasizing Value

This is achieved by highlighting the importance of the fundamental symmetry and relationship between suppliers and consumers. The surgeons and operating room staff will enhance the expertise of suppliers by providing input on the size, form and product packages. The importance of applying the Value Net strategy [2] lies in leveraging on the major fundamental **symmetry** between customers namely physicians in the hospital and suppliers. Along this vertical dimension, cooperation instead of competition will be emphasized with subsequent added value to both parties. We will also be examining the various dimensions in the application and usage of substitute products and or complementary ones. Light will be casted on the interplay between these last two along the horizontal dimension as well. See Fig. 7.2.

7.1.2 Mission of the S2P Project

The mission of the S2P project is to reduce cost of supplies and yet enhance their value in the operating room by surgical teams of various specialties.

Who is the team?
This project needs several resources and accessibility to data in order to succeed. Several players are essential in order to carry the mission of this project; These will be categorized along four stratums.

Surgeons: A key surgeon from each of the surgical departments will be nominated by the corresponding chair person to join the S2P project team
Operating Room Staff: Two staff from the operating room responsible for the supplies
Purchasing: A representative of the purchasing department
Billing: A representative of the billing department
Suppliers: A respresentative of the major suppliers once the key supplies are noted

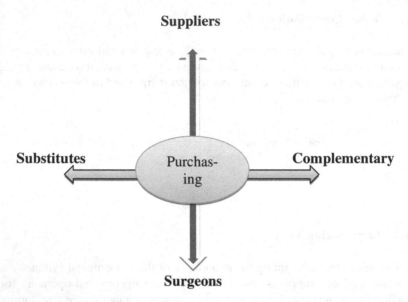

Fig. 7.2 The symmetric relationship between suppliers, surgeons, substitutes and complementary with purchasing at the center

Steps to follow:

1. Identify the 70 supplies most commonly used in the operating room
2. Identify the surgeons who use those supplies
3. List the procedures during which these supplies are used
4. Meet with the surgeons and operating nurses and dissect the mode of usage of these supplies and the variability in usage during the corresponding procedures
5. Identify with the surgeons the cost drivers and value drivers of each of these supplies with respect to the corresponding surgeries
6. Solicit a list of recommendations that may enhance the consumption of these supplies, reduce cost and add value to the final product
7. Discuss the recommendations with the operation managers and purchasing
8. Meet with the suppliers in order to agree on the implementation of the recommendations with special emphasis on the added value to both suppliers and consumers
9. Endorse the recommendations and tailor the changes in the supplies in order to match the needs of the surgeons and ultimately patient care
10. Negotiate the prices of the newly modified supplies.

7.2   The Nero Project

The basic principle of the Nero project is to reduce the bargaining power of suppliers by lowering their added value. Conventionally purchasing leverages on economy of scale to bargain with suppliers. A less intuitive approach is lowering the added value of the suppliers as reported by Brandenburger and Nalebuff [2].

The major operational initiatives to the application of this strategy in a hospital setting are listed below:

1. Meet with the purchasing department
2. Make a list of the supplies mostly used
3. Identify the corresponding major suppliers
4. Identify what percentage does the hospital represent of the total market share of each supplier,
5. Identify the hospital best alternative to negotiation agreement (BATNA) for each supplier
6. Compute the difference in costing
7. Re-negotiate your terms with the suppliers.

7.3   The Group Purchasing Project

With the rise in risk-based reimbursement, increase in cost and decrease in revenue, health systems are on the constant outlook to reduce cost. Being second to labor, supply cost may constitute up to 25% of the hospital bill thus making supply purchasing efficiency essential if the management plans to drive prices low [3].

Group purchasing organization is an entity used in many industries to help purchase supplies and needed material in a large scale with the purpose of reducing cost and getting marked discounts. Since its inception in 1910 by the Hospital Bureau of New York, it has been accessed by more than 90% of both profit and non-profit health organizations as well as acute and chronic care hospitals [4]. Their number has been stimulated in the early 70s by the Medicare Prospective Payment system which has led to their rapid expansion. The exchange of fee for service system by the PPS by the Federal government in 1980 where a given sum is paid for a patient with a particular diagnosis has urged hospitals and medical centers to find new means for cost reduction [5].

To that end, the purpose of the group purchasing project is to integrate the purchasing power of neighboring hospital and strategic allies, aggregate their purchasing volumes in order to do the purchasing at a group price and obtain volume discounts. This is achieved by leveraging the purchasing power of buyers to achieve discounts from the sellers. This Consolidation in the purchasing power allows healthcare providers to reduce cost of supplies up to 40% [6]. Not only with reduced expenses office efficiency is improved but also margin profits are higher. It starts by identifying and screening for the most commonly used supplies among the various stakeholders and develop a new purchasing strategy for negotiation, namely to pursue central sourcing and economy of scale. The span of products is not only limited to medical supplies but may also include medical devices and physician's preferred items, pharmaceuticals like vaccines, services such as communication, medical waste management, decision support analytics as well as savings on cost of processing credit and debit cards. Healthcare providers may also benefit in addition to the volume discounts from clinical support by having access to solutions to clinical problems and supply chain management. The supply chain management can reduce the backlog on purchasing orders, improve contract compliance and provide valuable information and cost analysis tools to better manage data and better reporting. Group purchasing organizations can also help in streamlining purchasing operations by assuring that contracts are accurate and non-deficient before proceeding with any order [7].

With respect to the management fees of the group purchasing organization, these are mainly administrative fees that are derived either from the suppliers or the vendors and can reach up to 3% of the total volume sale [8]. It is important to note that these fees are not contingent on the performance of the group or the amount of discount obtained. That being said, a main challenge is to pick up the right and most efficient group purchasing organization. In making that decision important points to consider are: Does this organization serve your market? In a sense how much your supplies constitute in terms of percentage their product portfolio and does this latter answers your needs and type of practice. A second important point is whether they do deliver significant reductions and cost savings and is their service good and reliable? A third important point is the presence of constraints and restrictions for your enrollment in this organization such as a given volume or annual membership fee [9].

7.4   Creation of Clinical Pathways and Guidelines

Clinical guidelines are well drafted protocols that aim at standardizing clinical practice thru the implementation of evidence based medicine. Based on the American Institute of Medicine, clinical guidelines are defined as "Systematically developed statements to assist practitioner and patient decisions about appropriate healthcare for specific clinical circumstances" [10]. These guidelines are developed by experts in specialized fields and or ad hoc committees in attempt to identify and recommend both diagnostic and therapeutic strategies in medical practice. These outlines for clinical practice act as guide not only to deliver and coordinate care among the multidisciplinary teams but also to monitor and review the outcome.

Clinical pathways are similar to clinical guidelines but are usually locally developed and are subject to close monitoring and constant change in the course of their implementation. Variations are allowed in these pathways which makes their effect on patient care more immediate and tangible. The proliferation of various guidelines and pathways has been attributed to several reasons, namely the large disparity in the number of surgeries in different areas with comparable demographics, the variation in expenses for the treatment of similar medical conditions, the increasing demand of third party payers for information to justify the billing of healthcare providers and last but not least is the linking of pay to performance with patient experience being central. Today more than 60% of hospitals in the United States have started clinical pathways with more than 20,000 health care standards and guidelines released [11, 12].

Though the development of clinical pathways stems from valid and legitimate reasons to improve healthcare and reduce cost, their implementation remains very challenging. The behavioral factors affecting adherence are complex to understand but can be summarized as follows; one is the abidance to "Cookbook Medicine" which is not well accepted by many physicians [13]. Many physicians are skeptical about clinical guidelines and believe that adopting these intervenes with their clinical freedom and doctor autonomy. A guideline that does not take into consideration the variability in clinical practice between primary care physicians and specialist, community practice and academic setting may well be resisted with little success in its implementation. Clinical guidelines need to be practical and easy to implement taking into consideration the variations in the need and setting of practices [14]. For example family physicians are more focused on treating symptoms rather than specific diagnosis, subsequently clinical guidelines developed for primary care physicians should relate to these practices [15]. A second factor affecting adherence to clinical guidelines is the fact that many of these guidelines are developed by national institutions and implemented locally without any tailoring to fit the norms of clinical practice within a given institution. Studies have shown that locally developed guidelines are more accepted and better implemented than national guidelines. On the other hand locally developed guidelines are constrained by the limited clinical, scientific time and managerial resources whereas nationally developed ones carry more scientific validity [16, 17]. Another cause for resistance is the questioning of the scientific validity of these guidelines by many practicing physicians. Though most guidelines are evidence based their implementation needs to be modified taking into consideration the context of practice locally within an institution. This local tailoring is crucial in order to circumvent any thoughts of threat or jeopardy by the local doctors. Another important limitation to the implementation of clinical guidelines is cost and its consequential effect on other budgets such as medication and overall cost of treatment. A challenge also is the "Burn-Out" of interest which is commonly encountered a short while after the development and introduction of a given guideline [18]. Frequent reminders and feedback on compliance rate and reports on patient outcome measures are key tools to foster the interest of physicians in pursuing these guidelines. Equally important challenge is overloading physicians with numerous guidelines in a short period of time. This overloading may cause major resistance and lack of compliance to these guidelines. Following a time strategy whereby not more than two guidelines are introduced yearly can mitigate this resistance and facilitate better compliance. Last but not least is the fear of using clinical guidelines for litigation purposes whereby failure to follow or abide to a given guideline for a particular disease may put the physician at risk of malpractice [19, 20].

Despite these challenges in introducing and developing clinical guidelines, many dissemination and implementation strategies have been developed to help their spread. These start by using social influence strategies such as interpersonal setting, persuasion setting using opinion leaders and mass media setting such as medical newspapers. Other important and commonly used tactics are: One is posting the guidelines in critical areas easily noticeable and accessible using posters, stickers or cards. Two is holding seminars that aim at introducing the newly set guidelines to physicians and healthcare providers. These seminars will not only highlight the content of these guidelines but will assist in their implementation. A third strategy to help dissemination is incorporating the guidelines within continuous medical education seminars and activities. This latter can be complemented by the usage of a facilitator that can help in explaining the content of these guidelines and their means of implementation. A fourth strategy is incorporating the guidelines into the computer system thus providing access to its content, tagging patient's records as well as facilitating auditing which again is a strategy by itself to monitor and provide feedback on compliance and adherence to guidelines [18, 21].

Irrespective of what implementation strategy is used to broaden the clinician's awareness regarding clinical guidelines, the impact should be on the attitudes and behavior of physicians as well as the resultant changes in health outcome measures [22].

It is worth noting that the impact of clinical guidelines on clinical outcomes has not yet been fully proven as most studies in the literature highlight the improvement in the process of care rather than medical outcome. A large review by Gimshaw in the evaluation of 91 studies on clinical guidelines revealed significant improvement in the processes of care in 81 and improvement in patient's outcome in only 12 [23]. A study by Emslie [24] on the impact of clinical guidelines in Scotland has lead to an improvement in the referral rate of infertility cases to specialists. Similarly a study conducted in England revealed that guidelines reduced the rate of inadequate or unindicated radiologic referrals [25]. On the other hand, in a systemic review by Graham Worrall on the effects of clinical practice guidelines on patient outcomes in primary care, only 5 out of 13 trials had statistically significant results. The most commonly treated conditions were hypertension, asthma and cigarette smoking, and the most commonly used dissemination strategies were computerized reminder systems, small group workshops and education sessions [26].

In a nutshell the effect of these guidelines on the implementation of clinical pathways reduces the variability in clinical practice and promotes organized and efficient patient care. It is one of the main tools to manage quality in a healthcare system concerned with standardization of care processes. It is a commonly used strategic tool that aims at reducing cost of clinical utilization given the finite resources available.

The main operational initiatives for the creation of clinical pathways are:

1. Dissection of common practices in each department and division
2. Aligning physician and management team interest
3. Identification of five clinical pathways by experienced clinicians within each department and division
4. Review the extent to which the clinical pathways are evidence based practice
5. Review the medical accuracy, ease of use and clinical applicability of these pathways
6. Study their impact on patient care, clinician's perspectives, prayer's perspectives, and administration.

The major strategic indicators are health outcome measures such as length of stay and complication rate, and financial indicators such as allowances for third party payers.

7.5   Patient Loyalty Program

Loyalty is not simply about the purchase and consumption of a service or product but about building a relationship with the consumer, a relationship that is based on the provision of a given need in a sustainable manner. The construct of this relationship lies on a thorough understanding of consumer's expectations and diligent attendance to meet those expectations. A single act of purchase is not a true reflection of loyalty as this can be the sequel to a geographic convenience; ease of accessibility, or simply to a personal acquaintance with a staff or faculty member within the institution. The presence of one's electronic medical record in a healthcare facility may also act as an incentive for a patient to visit repeatedly that facility without being loyal to it [27].

> For a healthcare provider keen on developing a self-sustained network of referrals, establishing a "Patient loyalty program" is a good initiative.

Several operational initiatives need be adopted and these include: The first operational initiative is defining the mission and objectives of the patient loyalty program. Though the theme might be similar in many institutions, each must carry a distinguished variation that harbors and support a unique identity. A mission statement of a given healthcare facility may emphasize the quest to transform every patient into an ambassador that carries the core value of this facility [28]. The second operational initiative lies in developing the "Home building metaphor" of the facility. This starts by answering the question "what distinguish our services from others in the market? And why should patients come to us and not to other healthcare facilities?". The answer to this question mandates a thorough dissection of the resources, capabilities and competencies of the institution in the context of patient's interest and care. Such a metaphor may be exemplified by a slogan to demonstrate that staff treats patients as family members [29]. This leads us to the third operational initiative and that is the identification of the model elements that can influence patient's behavior. This model element may lie in process efficiency, staff competencies, or may be embedded in routinization and needs further exploration. The fourth operational initiative is dissecting patient's value and perceptions in regard to the services provided. Understanding their preferences and perspectives is crucial not only for reform of the current practice but for the future delivery of new services. We have to remind ourselves that patient's experience that is key to medical practice nowadays, is the sum of many intersections and events in a patient's journey within a given facility, all of which influencing one's attitude and behavior either in a non-favorable manner leading to dissatisfaction or in a favorable manner leading to loyalty. That being said, patient's conduct is simply the percussion of his or her experience shaped by the various aforementioned inputs. Hence the program you chose should highlight and accentuate the brand image of the hospital and mostly fortify your relationship with your clients. This latter is mostly achieved by proper understanding of the purchasing behavior of the patient, as well as the patterns and trends in his relation with the hospital. Studying the purchasing habits of customers has been a very successful strategy used by Amazon and Google [30].

The fifth operational initiative is defining the means to accumulate points in the program. It is important to note that a patient loyalty program must not only convey additional value but also ensure that patients are coming back. Based on an article by Kendal Peiguss, there are seven programs that add value [31]. One is the simple points system where patients accumulate points with the purchase of any medical service in the institution. This program is mostly appreciated in businesses where there are frequent short and long term purchases. This can be achieved thru the consumption of different services such as laboratory, radiology, clinical services in addition to hospital admissions. In this program it is important to keep the addition and redeeming of points simple and intuitive. A good example is Boloco in the food industry [32]. Another important program is using the Tier system, which helps achieve the balance between what is attainable and what is desired in terms of rewards. In this program patients are stratified as either bronze, silver or gold based on the time of their enrollment so that those who enroll initially have an increasing value of their rewards [33].

Though the time between purchase and redeeming should not matter still it is preferable to shorten the time between purchase and gratification. A good example of this program is Virgin Airlines.

The last initiative of patient loyalty program lies in proper management of the program and designing means to redeem the accumulated points. The purpose of this initiative is to increase the percentage of loyal patients by managing their basic needs, addressing what matters the most to them, and delivering services in a consistent and reliable manner.

> The key question is "What should we offer?" is it a discount with every second purchase, is it a bonus or free item, is it accumulating points, or is it a VIP treatment?

There are numerous ways to redeem points such as upgrades, special line for check in, and access to non-medical services, discounts and so forth. An intuitive way to build more customers is to "structure non-monetary programs around your customer's value" [34]. This is achievable in medical practice by looking at the activities the patient is enrolled in while seeking a medical service. This can range from transportation service to lodging among other intersects in his/her journey as a patient. This can be facilitated by partnering with other companies such as hotels, restaurants and retails shops. For VIP patients, an upfront charge may help expedite certain barriers between the patient and your business as hospital. An example would be a fast lane for checking in, access to medical information, an upgrade in admission. Whatever program you chose, it should be well communicated to the clients using several communication arms such as social media, newsletters and word of mouth.

7.6   Physician Integration Strategy

With the increase in turbulence of the healthcare environment, namely the cost containment policies and the advent of prospective payment, there has been a growing interest to strengthen the relationship between physicians and hospital administrators. A very obvious reason is the major role that practitioners play in determining the usage of hospital resources in their practice, with the subsequent impact on cost and expenditures within the healthcare system. Based on a review by [35], physicians by controlling the number of admissions, mode of therapy and length of stay, affect up to 80% of health care expenditures. Hence there is "—growing demand for change—" in the relationship between physicians and hospitals as reported by the American College of Healthcare Executives [36] and a drastic need to align physician's interest with that of medical institutions.

To this end, various physician integration strategies have been developed in attempt to reduce the strain between physicians' goals and those of administrators.

> The two major core notions behind these strategies are; one, closer tightening of the interest of the two parties financially and psychologically thru the build of enhanced trust with subsequent loyalty and greater control of cost.

This latter is achieved by improving the cooperation of physicians in containing expenditures in their medical decisions and improving utilization of resources, and two by creating added value for both parties. This latter is primarily derived from the synergy in meshing the expertise and managerial skills of both, as a result of which, physicians professionalism plays a major role in administrative decisions and the making of organizational objectives [37].

> With these core notions in mind, it is obvious that physician integration is a mul-
> tifaceted and complex construct that is closely tied to other constructs such as
> physician trust and collaboration, physician alignment, physician commitment and
> physician leadership.

In the adoption of any physician integration strategy, the focus will be on developing means and tactics that enable physicians to engage more efficiently in managing quality in a cost-effective manner. The main goal will be obviously to reach a balance between cost of patient care and quality.

Before embarking in the description of the different physician integration strategies, it is important to describe the operational initiatives towards the implementation of these strategies. This starts with a better understanding of the differences between healthcare managers and physicians perspectives on power, economic and non-economic integration in medical practice [38]. It is not uncommon to witness physicians adopting a procrastination strategy as a tactic to avert managerial meetings, to delay the implementation of strategic projects and to deter from providing data for critical managerial projects. Similarly, strategic ambiguity is often pursuit in communication with physicians by declining to provide clinical evidence for a given practice, refusing to follow clinical protocols or over criticizing managerial decisions [39]. Physicians are primarily concerned with patient's health outcome whereas managers worry about the overall patient experience, a statement often heard by many practitioners to describe the disparity in opinion among the two regarding patient care [40].

In order to mitigate that disparity we need to follow the second and third operational initiatives, namely to understand what physicians want to hear from the administration and to define the determinants of physician engagement, in other words, what does it take to have them on board. Physicians want to hear from the leaders of the institution words of confidence on the organization's success in relation to patient's satisfaction and overall performance. They also mandate acts of respect and care towards their practice and persons. Feeling that the organization cares about its faculty and treats them with respect is a key mandate to have physicians on board. Defining the determinants of physician engagement is a major challenge. These determinants can be either job related or based on personal queries. Job related determinants can include extending the level of autonomy, widening their task identity, assuming an administrative or financial position, the need for a more thorough feedback on the practice of the institution. Personal determinants can be self-efficacy and personal optimism. The fourth initiative is the development and adoption of one or many models that facilitate physician engagement. The model should be based on active listening of what physicians want [41].

With these operational initiatives in mind, three main physician integration strategies have been described. One is involving physicians in hospital governance thru decision making programs and policy level decisions [42, 43]. This form of integration peaked in the early 1980 and is based on hospital board restructuring with many benefits to it among which are control over policy decisions and creating uniformity in cultures and homogeneity in the working environment. Another benefit to this shared governance strategy is the increased level of physician's cost consciousness. Once on board and taking financial decisions, physicians start sharing fiduciary responsibilities with administrators and thus become more concerned about cost and expenditures. They are also more likely to adapt to administrative decisions and collaborate more in the process of enhancing profitability and occupancy. A study by James B on the effects of hospital integration strategies on hospital performance revealed that the impact of having physicians on board is mostly pronounced on profitability and rate of admissions and less on cost practice and reduction [37]. These benefits on the other hand may be offset by unnecessary expenditures such as high salaries and monetary compensations. That is why it is important to limit the extent of physicians' involvement to not more than 30% of the board complement [44].

Another less commonly used strategy is thru direct ownership. This integration strategy puts both physicians and administrators on the same platform, sharing same risks and benefits. It also gives more opportunity to widen the capital by soliciting more investors in healthcare. Despite the aforementioned advantages, this form of strategy has declined markedly because of the new regulatory and financial constraints in healthcare in many countries, which made the investment in hospitals less attractive. Again in the study by James B, this form of strategy associated with lower occupancy rates and reduced operating margins [37].

Other forms of integration strategies are the financial ones [45]. Financial Integration strategies range from renting facilities, providing managerial functions to physicians, providing contracting services, allowing joint ventures, and last but not least is physician employment. As mentioned repetitively by physicians, having a steady and secure income is a major concern. The fee for service model has been an insecure payment model especially given the value-based aspect of medical care. In view of this declining traditional financial model, namely fee-for-service, and the rising sentiment of dissatisfaction of physicians regarding revenue and securing a fixed well compensated income, new alignment and integration models came to picture. Models that first and foremost address the need for fair physician compensation should also meet the growing demands of the healthcare environment for broad medical services, value-based performance and cost-efficiency. These models need also to meet the changes in market demands, and the avoidance of excessive financial burdens as a sequel to salaried positions.

Any new model of employment should ensure sustained productivities thru the introduction of incentives and compensation agreements, and should provide forums that enable physicians to voice their thoughts in critical decision making matters thus creating a win-win formula for both parties. As such, compensation agreements are gaining traction as value-based payment methodologies to reward quality and efficiency. These are being adopted by many health care institutes in attempt to manage their population in a coordinated matter. The main challenges in adopting an employed setting for physicians are determining the right amount of compensation, sustaining productivity, aligning physicians' vision and strategy with those of the institution, defining quality and efficiency metrics, and creating the right incentives financial and non-financial to ensure commitment and long term continuity. The amount of compensation can be determined using three essential steps based on [46]; one is computing the average income over the last three years inclusive of billing records and taxes, two is comparing the computed average to the current income of the group of same specialty in the institution as a benchmark; three is structuring the compensation plan based on the projected productivity of the physician using either relative value unit or revenue as a tool, along with an incentive plan that feeds towards it. It is important to note that physicians have little or no control on collection and revenue which favors linking the compensation plan to amount of productivity rather than to revenue. Any compensation plan may face the dreadful possibility of decrease in revenue once physicians are employed. Based on a survey by [46] in 2014, 56% of physicians had a slight decrease and 29% had a substantial decrease in productivity. Accordingly it is highly recommended that once physicians move to an employed setting, to have the compensation plan coupled with an incentive model. The incentive model coupled to any compensation plan should be linked to the different incentive metrics that are integral to the mission of the institution. Such metrics can include, quality of care be it clinical, managerial or patient experience, system performance in terms of efficiency as in cost-to-service ratio and patient load, utilization of resources as in volume in relation to capacity, accessibility, research, teaching and others. An example is the OSF healthcare "transitional compensation model" where 80% of compensation is linked to productivity and 20% to incentive metrics [47]. The main challenge is defining those metrics, implementing these and auditing the outcome. These need to be meaningful, valid and accurate, truly reflective of quality and team-based care, and most of all well communicated and adopted by physicians.

Other form of financial programs between physicians and hospitals is the gain sharing program. This latter as defined by Schuster [48] is "designed to share the benefits of improved productivity, cost reductions and quality in the form of regular cash payouts" in contrary to compensation practices where a percentage of the profit is usually shared with the employees. A study by Paul E. Juras entitled "An analysis of gain sharing in a health care setting" showed that this kind of financial program did not have a favorable effect on hospital productivity, which questions the validity in adopting such a program [49].

Though the financial incentive is a mandate to improve quality of service and sustain productivity, it is not enough to keep physicians' productivity aligned with the strategic goals of the institution. Aside from revenue, for physicians to commit to high standard practice and care delivery, they need to be further engaged. According to Ulhum of Healthcare Strategy Group, in addition to the provision of financial stability, there has to be a culture of shared vision and objectives, driven by a team of physicians assuming leadership and governance positions with a focus on process improvement and better quality of care [50].

Other forms of financial integration strategies is building strategic alliances thru co-management agreements, provision of management services, and creating clinically integrated network [51]. Once a hospital has proven a track record in managing private practices, it can use its competency to provide administrative services to group practicing physicians or other healthcare providers. It can also provide C0-management agreements whereby these types of agreements are reserved for specialty practices that wish to benefit from hospital management to improve their operational efficiencies and outcome yet remain independent.

On the other hand, Clinically Integrated networks are forms of alignment between hospitals and physicians who wish to remain independent. For hospitals it is a form of alignment between the two parties that provides a platform for collaboration without the financial cost of full employment. For physicians it is a kind of arrangement that aims at improving their efficiency and quality of care, modify their practice patterns and improve their revenue by jointly contracting with payers and health plans. Accountable Care Organization ACO is a form of Clinically Integrated Networks that focus on managing population by providing coordinated care and yet reducing cost. It may take many forms along a wide spectrum that ranges between Full-spectrum Integrated ACO to Physician group alliance to hospital alliance ACOs [52].

Other forms include physicians-hospital organizations/Integrated systems, Management service organization MSO by Burns and Thorpe 1993, and Strategic alliances between hospitals and physicians Gregory 1992.

7.7 Physician Liaison Program

The main goal of health care providers is to sustain good quality thru evidence-based-practices and to maintain a financially sound benefit/cost ratio by focusing on primary care medicine and by shifting to value-based payments. In the implementation of these objectives, hospitals must navigate smartly in the community and within its premises. The challenge is to be able to collaborate with healthcare stakeholders rather than compete with them, and to subsequently sustain and expand ones market share. To that end, physician liaison program is one of the strategic tactics used by many healthcare providers in attempt to widen their network and reach out for new referrals. Based on the "American Association of Physician Liaisons", the mission is to "—*advance the art of physician and healthcare provider relationships through the provision of educational programming, professional development, shared resources and networking opportunities*" [53]. Hence, the physician liaison program is intended to strengthen the relationship between physicians, hospitals and other medical facilities. Patients must be satisfied with the standard of care, care provision must be well balanced between cost-effectiveness and quality, and last but not least referring physicians must be compensated and incentivized. This latter lies primarily in securing steady financial resources with sound acknowledgment of the role of physicians and staff as decision makers and practitioners in healthcare.

Now in order to have this win-win collaboration strategy between the three main stakeholders in healthcare, namely physicians, patients and hospitals, the physician liaison program must be built on three main constructs [54].

The first construct resides in identifying the current market share of the given institution and defending its boundaries by securing proper physician referrals. This is done by ensuring that patients referred to and within the institution are contented with the standard of care and by communicating the patient's contentment to the referring physician. The second construct lies in identifying new market segments and targets and in ensuring new retention strategies that overcome the competitiveness of other healthcare providers. The third construct is a sequel to the first two and lies on improving the utilization of the institution resources. The main challenge is to maintain synergy among the three aforementioned stakeholders and make sure that a collaborative rather than a competitive mind set dominates the rules of the game.

Today Physician liaison is essential for the survival of many hospitals that rely on physician's referrals for their patient base. Despite the integral role of referring physician in securing the load of patients to these hospitals, the outreach strategies are often underdeveloped if present at all. Most of marketing is directed towards specific programs or services thus masking physician's network as a core competency to any medical institution [55]. Managers often complain of limited growth in load and revenue, yet the referring channels are not well maintained and nourished. This brings us to the need of marketing towards physician and staff who send their patients to a given health care provider. By marketing we are not only referring to outreach policies and promotion tactics but also to building a relationship well sustained on trust, transparency and the well-being of patients. To this end, physician liaison program serves to not only increase patient referrals, but also develop and maintain a healthy relationship with the referring physicians and solicit new referral sources and secure new businesses to the institution. Add to the importance of maintaining and nourishing the body of referring physician as a main goal, physician liaison program also aims at improving patient care [56]. This latter is achieved thru the enhanced communication between the referring physician and the treating ones, thru easy access to the services required, and the provision of timely reports (radiology and laboratory results and follow up notes). More so, this program will address in efficient manner any negative feedback or flaws in the patient experience throughout the referral.

Other conventional methods used in physician liaison programs are: referring physician directories, newsletters to referring physicians, birthday letters, sharing academic activities such as CME courses, hospital events and community service events, and less frequently direct visits to doctors and face to face encounters [57]. The rationale behind this latter is to foster the personal contact between the two because most studies agree that physicians are more likely to refer to physicians that they know and have encountered before. In addition to these traditional marketing vehicles used in physician liaison, comes the social marketing and netting. Based on numerous research studies, physicians are joining social networks more and more and "85% maintain their broadband in their offices" based on Manhattan research study published in 2009 [58]. That being said, it is imperative to use social networks and other forms of social media to connect with physicians in addition to the classical means of marketing. Physician relation program cannot excel if it does not embed social networking and digital communication. Dan Dunlop, president Jennings, has recommended steps that can be followed to achieve this new form of netting. It starts by engaging physicians on a "Physician-only social network" [59], a network made accessible only to physicians. This platform for communication will resemble the "Doctor's lounge" [57], a place to share experience and discuss cases, all to the benefit of patient care. That same social network will also allow the advertisement and promotion of the core competencies and unique services of the department or division promoted. Using twitters and other social media tools such as blogs, a large network can be developed and physicians will be able to interact in a seamless rather than interruptive manner, and discuss medical cases.

Equally important to these conventional physician liaison methods and their complementary products using social netting is to have the house in order, meaning to say, to be able to assimilate the increase in load and serve the newly referred patient's base in a timely and efficient manner. That being said, it is essential to have three key elements prior to any outreach effort to solicit new referrals; one is accessibility, two is good service, and three is adequate follow up of the patient and timely feedback to the referring physician.

7.8 Staff Engagement Program

Embarking on a competitive landscape where patient satisfaction and cost effectiveness became intertwined, managers have to engage their staff at all fronts. It is a fact nowadays that staff and employees are the primary internal stakeholders and contributors to the delivery of the vision and mission of the institution. When growth in the workforce and capacity is the primary objective, service design and staff engagement become essential components to any reform. By increasing the workforce engagement of any institution, there is development of new integrated health care programs. This is achieved by aligning competencies with job requirements, incorporating new roles, and proper staff training and development. All the aforementioned leads to improvement in productivity and performance, fosters retention and sustain differentiation and innovation. Hence staff engagement is commonly used as a strategic tactic towards service differentiation and cost reduction, with numerous reports linking staff engagement to quality of care provided, patient satisfaction, mortality and morbidity rates, as well as financial performance [1].

To that end, staff engagement has become a core value for the survival and growth of any enterprise, more so in healthcare. It is about having the interest of the institution at heart and believing that he or she can make a difference. It is about caring for the values and mission of the institution with a strong attachment to the daily experiences at work. In other words, it is Hybrid of emotional attachment and rational belief, that positions staff as an integral element of the organization where his or her contribution makes a difference. This enthusiasm to work and willingness to cross the Rubicon in achieving a task when requested mandates a mutual and symmetrical relationship between managers and employees. In healthcare, it is witnessed in the management and thrives to improve patient's satisfaction. Based on the National Health Service Staff engagement toolkit, engagement results from a number of factors: One is "delivering great management and leadership", two "promoting a healthy and safe work environment", three" supporting personal development and training", four, enabling involvement in decision-making, and five "ensuring every role counts" [2]. Other equally important means of engagement are equity in dealing with the different staff, transparency in the management, provision of an accessible platform for timely communication, and last but not least is encouragement of employees to voice their thoughts and challenge routinization. This can be achieved by having and sharing the clear vision of the institution, by securing the right channels for communication, by ensuring the well-being of the staff, by nourishing a culture of collaboration and team spirit, a culture that acknowledges personal achievements, celebrates milestones and rewards employees, favors exploration aside from exploitation, provides time flexibility, favors collaboration and perfects the on boarding of new employees [3]. A healthy working environment is one that encourages the visibility of its staff, values traits of excellence, attitude of loyalty, and rewards great achievements. On the other hand, staff needs to reciprocate this outreach engagement strategy by coming forward when challenges rise, by meeting the deadlines for deliverables, and by putting the interest of the organization first and foremost in any job requested. Employees must believe in the mission of the organization and feel the urge and need to be part of it by committing to it.

> In a nutshell, staff engagement mandates a thorough examination of the current staff situation using various surveys or group discussions, evaluation of the performance and appraisal processes, revisiting of the current surveys used for assessment, and possibly the development of new electronic platforms to enhance communication.

Subsequently several initiatives need to be taken in relation to workforce, recruitment, performance management, leadership development as well as training and development. In brief these include having a favorable working environment, a platform for communication among staff and between staff and managers, implementation of the staff feedback, alignment between the job requirements and staff competencies, and last but not least is heartfelt engagement.

References

1. Normann, R. and Ramirez, R., 1993. From value chain to value constellation. *Harvard business review*, *71*(4), pp. 65–77.
2. Brandenburger, AM. and Nalebuff, BJ. (1995), 'The Right Game: Use Game Theory to Shape Strategy', *Harvard Business Review*, 73(4): 57–71.
3. Massachusetts Hospital Association, 2010. Hospital costs in context: a transparent view of the cost of care. *Burlington: Massachusetts Hospital Association*. Available at: Hospital Costs in Context: A Transparent View of the Cost of Care www.mhalink.org/AM/TemplateRedirect. cfm?Template=/CM/.
4. Guerin-Calvert, M.E., Israilevich, G. and Lexecon, C., 2011. Assessment of cost trends and price differences for US hospitals. *American Hospital Association. Retrieved June, 12*, p. 2012.
5. Guterman, S. and Dobson, A., 1986. *Impact of the Medicare prospective payment system for hospitals*. Health Care Financing Administration. Available at: Impact of the Medicare prospective payment system for hospitals www.ncbi.nlm.nih.gov/pmc/articles/PMC4191526
6. Go, A.S., Mozaffarian, D., Roger, V.L., Benjamin, E.J., Berry, J.D., Blaha, M.J., Dai, S., Ford, E.S., Fox, C.S., Franco, S. and Fullerton, H.J., 2013. AHA statistical update. *Circulation*, *127*, pp.e62-e245. Available at: A 2014 Update of Cost Savings and Marketplace Analysis of the... https://c.ymcdn.com/sites/.../hsca_cost_savings_group_purc. pdf
7. Sink, H.L., Langley Jr, C.J. and Gibson, B.J., 1996. Buyer observations of the US third-party logistics market. *International Journal of Physical Distribution & Logistics Management*, *26* (3), pp. 38–46. Available at: The Pros and Cons of Group Purchasing Organizations, by Janine... hotelexecutive.com/.../the-pros-and-cons-of-group-purchasing-organizations.
8. Group purchasing organization. (2015, June). Retrieved September 06, 2016. Available at: Group purchasing organization - Wikipedia, the free encyclopedia https://en.wikipedia.org/ wiki/Group_purchasing_organization
9. Why become a supplier with Premier? (n.d.). Retrieved September 06, 2016. Available at: Selecting a group purchasing organization: Supplier partners https://www.premierinc.com/ supplier-partners/why-premier/
10. Institute of Medicine, 1990. Clinical practice guidelines. Washington: National Academy Press.
11. Leone A., 1993. Medical practice guidelines are useful tools in litigation. Med Malpractice; 10:1.
12. Giffin M, Giffin R B., 1994. Critical pathways produce tangible results. Health Care Strategic Management; 12:17–23.
13. Woolf SH. 1992Practice guidelines, a new reality in medicine. Methods of developing guidelines. Arch Intern Med; 152:946–952.
14. Grimshaw, J.M. and Russel, I.T., 1994. Implementing clinical practice guidelines: can guidelines be used to improve clinical practice. *Effective Health Care, 8*, pp. 1–12.

15. Hopkins, A., 1995. Some reservations about clinical guidelines. *Archives of disease in childhood*, 72(1), pp. 70–75.
16. North of England Study of Standards and Performance in General Practice, 1992. Medical audit in general practice: effect on doctors; clinical behavior and the health of patients with common childhood conditions. BMJ; 304: 480–8.
17. Grimshaw, J. and Russell, I., 1993. Achieving health gain through clinical guidelines. I: Developing scientifically valid guidelines. *Quality in health care*,2(4), p. 243–248
18. Forrest, D., Hoskins, A. and Hussey, R., 1996. Clinical guidelines and their implementation. *Postgraduate medical journal*, 72(843), pp. 19–22.
19. Lomas J, Anderson GM, Dominic-Pierre K, et al, 1989. Do practice guidelines guide practice? The effect of a consensus statement on the practice of physicians. N Engl J Med; 321: 1306–1311
20. Clark, C.M. and Kinney, E.D., 1994. The potential role of diabetes guidelines in the reduction of medical injury and malpractice claims involving diabetes. *Diabetes Care*, 17(2), pp. 155–159.
21. Stocking, B., 1992. Promoting change in clinical care. *Quality in Health Care*, 1(1), p. 56–60.
22. Conroy, M. and Shannon, W., 1995. Clinical guidelines: their implementation in general practice. *Br J Gen Pract*, 45(396), pp. 371–375.
23. Grimshaw, J., Freemantle, N., Wallace, S., Russell, I., Hurwitz, B., Watt, I., Long, A. and Sheldon, T., 1995. Developing and implementing clinical practice guidelines. *Quality in Health care*, 4(1), p. 55.
24. Emslie C, Grimshaw J, Templeton A., 1993. Do clinical guidelines improve general practice management and referral of infertile couples? *BMJ*; 306:1728–31.
25. Royal College of Radiologists Working Party, 1993. Influence of guidelines on referral from general practice. *BMJ*; 306:110–1.
26. Worrall, G., Chaulk, P. and Freake, D., 1997. The effects of clinical practice guidelines on patient outcomes in primary care: a systematic review.*Canadian Medical Association Journal*, 156(12), pp. 1705–1712.
27. Boshoff, C. and Gray, B., 2004. The relationships between service quality, customer satisfaction and buying intentions in the private hospital industry. *South African Journal of Business Management*, 35(4). Available at: The relationships between service quality, customer satisfaction and buying intentions in the private hospital industry.
28. Macstravic, R.S., 1994. Hospital patient loyalty: causes and correlates. *Journal of hospital marketing*, 8(2), pp. 67–72
29. Brocato, J. J., & Mavis, B. (2005). The research productivity of faculty in family medicine departments at US medical schools: a national study. *Academic Medicine*, 80(3), 244–252.
30. Building Customer Loyalty the Hard (And Only) Way, 2013. Retrieved September 06, 2016. Available at: Building Customer Loyalty the Hard (And Only) Way - Forbes, www.forbes.com/.../building-customer-loyalty-the-hard-and-only-way/
31. Rewards Visa Card. (n.d.). Retrieved September 06, 2016. Available at: Amazon.com Shop with Points www.amazon.com/points
32. Kolowich, L. (2015). 7 Customer Loyalty Programs That Actually Add Value. Retrieved September 06, 2016. Available at: 7 Customer Loyalty Programs That Actually Add Value - HubSpot, blog.hubspot.com/.../7-Customer-Loyalty-Programs-That-Actually-Add-Value. aspx
33. Peiguss, K. 7 Customer Loyalty Programs That Actually Add Value.
34. McEachern, A. (2014). Tiered Programs, Why They Are Great For Customer Loyalty. Retrieved September 06, 2016. Available at: Tiered Programs, Why They Are Great For Customer Loyalty https://www.sweettoothrewards.com/blog/tiered-program-loyalty/
35. Chilingerian, J.A. and Sherman, H.D., 1990. Managing physician efficiency and effectiveness in providing hospital services. *Health Services Management Research*, 3(1), pp. 3–15.
36. Arthur Andersen, and the American College of Healthcare Executives, 1991. *The Future of Healthcare: Physician and Hospital Relationships. Chicago.*

37. Goes, J.B. and Zhan, C., 1995. The effects of hospital-physician integration strategies on hospital financial performance. *Health Services Research, 30*(4), p. 507.
38. Waldman, J.D. and Cohn, K.H., 2008. Mending the gap between physicians and hospital executives. [In Cohn KH, Houg D, eds] *The Business of Healthcare*, pp. 27–57
39. Chervenak, F.A., McCullough, L.B. and Schmitz, V., 2003. Physicians and hospital managers as cofiduciaries of patients: Rhetoric or reality?/Practitioner application. *Journal of Healthcare Management, 48*(3), p. 172.
40. Kaissi, A., 2005. Manager-physician relationships: an organizational theory perspective. *The health care manager, 24*(2), pp. 165–176.
41. Kaissi, A.A., 2012. A roadmap for trust: enhancing physician engagement. *Canadian Policy Network.*
42. Montague, J., 1993. Straight talk. Doctor-driven systems tell how they've gained physician allies. *Hospitals & health networks/AHA, 67*(13), pp. 22–27.
43. Morlock, L.L., Alexander, J.A. and Hunter, H.M., 1985. Formal relationships among governing boards, CEOs, and medical staffs in independent and system hospitals. *Medical Care, 23*(10), pp. 1193–1213.
44. Starkweather, D., 1988. Hospital board power. *Health Services Management Research, 1*(2), pp. 74–86.
45. Morrisey, M.A., Alexander, J.A. and Ohsfeldt, R.L., 1990. Physician integration strategies and hospital output: A comparison of rural and urban institutions. *Medical Care*, pp. 586–603.
46. An HFMA Value Project Report: Phase 3, 2014. Strategies for Physician Engagement and Alignment. Healthcare Financial Management Association 3 Westbrook Corporate Center, Westchester, IL. Internet Source
47. Taitz, J. M., Lee, T. H., & Sequist, T. D. (2011). A framework for engaging physicians in quality and safety. *BMJ quality & safety*, bmjqs-2011.
48. Schuster, M., 1986. "Gainsharing: The State of the Art." Compensation and Benefits Management 2, no. 4 p. 285–90
49. Juras, P.E., Kaspin, J. and Martin, D.R., 1994. An analysis of gainsharing in a health care setting. *The Health Care Manager, 13*(2), pp. 44–50.
50. Denis, J. L. (2013). *Exploring the dynamics of physician engagement and leadership for health system improvement prospects for Canadian* (Doctoral dissertation, École nationale d'administration publique).
51. Gregory, D., 1992. Strategic alliances between physicians and hospitals in multihospital systems. *Journal of Healthcare Management, 37*(2), p. 247.
52. Shortell, S. M., Wu, F. M., Lewis, V. A., Colla, C. H., & Fisher, E. S. (2014). A taxonomy of accountable care organizations for policy and practice. *Health services research, 49*(6), 1883–1899.
53. Home page of the website of American Association of Physician liaison program, n.d.
54. Implementing a Physical Liaison Program, 2015. Partnership, Physician compensation, Physician Productivity, Referrals, By Amanda Chay
55. PHYSICIAN LIAISON REFERRAL MARKETING GROWS YOUR REFERRAL PATIENT VOLUME. (n.d.). Retrieved September 06, 2016. Available at: Physician Liaison Referral Marketing - Physician Referral Marketing physicianreferralmarketing.com/physician-liaison-marketing/
56. Kripalani, S., LeFevre, F., Phillips, C.O., Williams, M.V., Basaviah, P. and Baker, D.W., 2007. Deficits in communication and information transfer between hospital-based and primary care physicians: implications for patient safety and continuity of care. *Jama, 297*(8), pp. 831–841. Available at: [HTML] Deficits in communication and information transfer between hospital-based and primary care physicians: implications for patient safety and continuity of care, S Kripalani, F LeFevre, CO Phillips, MV Williams…—Jama, 2007—archpsyc.jamanetwork.com
57. Dan Dunlop, 2011. Marketing to the Social Physician, by, Issue 1. Marketing for better health.

58. Cooper, C.P., Gelb, C.A., Rim, S.H., Hawkins, N.A., Rodriguez, J.L. and Polonec, L., 2012. Physicians who use social media and other internet-based communication technologies. *Journal of the American Medical Informatics Association*, *19*(6), pp. 960–964. Available at: Physicians who use social media and other internet-based communication technologies CP Cooper, CA Gelb, SH Rim...—Journal of the ..., 2012—jamia.oxfordjournals.org

59. Dan Dunlop, 2010. Marketing to referring Physicians: A Largely Untapped Opportunity, Healthcare Marketing Report.

60. Safran, D. G., Taira, D. A., Rogers, W. H., Kosinski, M., Ware, J. E., & Tarlov, A. R. (1998). Linking primary care performance to outcomes of care.*Journal of Family Practice*, *47*(3), 213–221.

61. MacLeod, D., & Clarke, N. (2010). Leadership and employee engagement: passing fad or a new way of doing business?. *International Journal of Leadership in Public Services*, *6*(4), 26–30.

62. Bandarin, F., Hosagrahar, J., & Sailer Albernaz, F. (2011). Why development needs culture. *Journal of Cultural Heritage Management and Sustainable Development*, *1*(1), 15–25.

Chapter 8
Application of Porter's Strategies in Lebanese Hospitals

Porter's generic strategies, namely cost leadership and differentiation, have been described thoroughly in the literature as dominant typologies adopted by many firms in various industries, among which is healthcare [1, 2]. The performance of hospitals has been shown to differ markedly in accordance with the degree of environment-organization fit. Consequently changes in the adoption of the various generic strategies in different contexts have been shown to vary. Hospitals with appropriate "strategy-environment combination" outperformed those with less of a combination [3]. Hence to change the type of strategy while adapting to environmental discontinuities is crucial for hospitals performance. These environmental discontinuities are exemplified by several dramatic changes such as the introduction of prospective payments, introduction of new technologies and more.

There are only two reports on the applicability of Porter's strategies in hospital settings, one by Kumar et al. on hospitals in the United States hospitals and the other by Hlavacka et al. on Slovak hospital industry [4, 5]. The first study by Kumar et al. performed on 600 acute care hospitals looked at the types of strategies used by chief administrators and how these strategies correlated with performance. Five groups of strategies have been reported and traditional performance criteria were used as measure of organizational performance. The five types of strategies included cost leaders, differentiators, stuck in the middle, focused cost leaders and focused differentiators. With respect to performance, return on new services and facilities, ability to retain patients and to control expenditure was used as measures of effectiveness and efficiency. The second study by Hlavacka was conducted on Slovak hospitals using a translated version of Kumar's questionnaire. Again their findings indicated four types of strategy, namely the focused cost leadership, the stuck in the middle, the "wait and see group" which had medium emphasis on cost leadership and low emphasis on focus and differentiation, and last but not least is cost leadership. The results showed that the "stuck in the middle" performed better that the remaining groups.

No previous study has reported the types of strategies used in Lebanese hospitals and their impact on performance. Given the importance of the environment as a

© The Author(s) 2017
A. L. Hamdan, *Strategic Thinking in a Hospital Setting*,
SpringerBriefs in Public Health, DOI 10.1007/978-3-319-53597-5_8

context for the application of any strategy, and given the disparities in the healthcare systems across different countries and the impact of the socio-economical and political factors on healthcare providers in general, the applicability of Porter's generic strategies in Lebanese hospitals is reported in this chapter. The outcome of this investigation will either refute or substantiate the viability of these strategies in a very turbulent and discontinuous environment, namely that of Lebanon. The descriptive analysis will also be correlated with the extent of performance of these hospitals, in particular vis-à-vis patient's experience and ability to retain patients.

The purpose of this investigation is; (1) to Identify the types of strategies used in Lebanese hospitals, low-cost leadership, versus service differentiation, versus hybrid form often referred to as dual competitive strategy, (2) to investigate the performance of these hospitals with respect to quality of care, and (3) to analyze the correlation between the different types of strategies and levels of quality of care.

This prospective study was performed using a variation on a modified questionnaire initially described by Kumar et al. [5]. The questionnaire that was used consisted of 13 close ended questions that shed information on the type of strategy used and the performance of hospitals investigated. The questionnaire was sent to 60 hospitals in Lebanon located in different geographic areas in order for the sample to be representative of the Lebanese hospitals as a whole. The questionnaires were delivered by hand to the chief administrator after having been informed by phone (personal contact) about the purpose of this investigation. One of the possible shortcoming or limitation of this study is the small sample size and the restricted cooperation by some of the chief administrators.

8.1   Material and Method

A total of 60 questionnaires were distributed to chief administrators of 60 hospitals in Lebanon. For the purpose of this study a modified version of the Kumar et al. questionnaire was used [5]. The questionnaire is a subjective tool to assess the type of strategy used and its relation to performance. Previous study substantiates the use of subjective measures as an alternative to objective ones. The correlation between the two types of measurements was greater than 0.01, which strongly favors the usage of subjective questions when objective measurements are absent or not shared publically [6].

The questionnaire had three components to it. The first component is on demographic variables, namely number of beds and location, rural versus urban. We have elected not to include profit versus non-profit status because of lack of transparency and inaccessibility to such information. The second component of the questionnaire is on the type of strategy used. For the differentiation strategy, three questions were asked: "Introduce new services", "Differentiate existing services", "Utilizing market research to introduce new services". For the low-cost leadership strategy six questions were asked: "Achieving lower cost of services than competitors", "making services more cost efficient", "Improving the time and cost required for co-ordination of various services", "Improving the utilization of available staff, equipment, services and facilities", "Performing an analysis of costs associated with various services", "Improving availability of diagnostic equipment and auxiliary services to control costs". Subjects were asked to indicate the extent to which their institution is engaged in the above competitive activities: 1 = indicates the least engagement and 7 = the most engagement.

The third component is regarding performance. The original questionnaire by Kumar, Subramanian and Yauger included three conventional measures, namely "return on new services/facilities and profit margin", "retaining patients" and "success in controlling expenses" [5]. In this study in order to assess performance we have elected to use quality as one of the six intermediate outcome measures described by Bradley et al. [7] in their HNP Discussion paper "Developing Strategies for improving Health care delivery". We have excluded absolute and numerical performance measures because these are usually either unavailable or not displayed publically.

Based on Webster definition [8], quality is defined as "a distinctive inherent feature" or "a degree of excellence" (Webster's Third New International Dictionary, 1993) whereas in healthcare it is defined as "doing the right thing at the right time, in the right way, for the right person and having the best possible results" [9]. Another definition of quality by the Institute of Medicine (2001) states that "Quality of care is the degree to which health services for individuals and populations increase the likelihood of desired health outcomes and are consistent with current professional knowledge" [10]. In both definitions there is a focus on outcome of care as perceived by the patient and on professionalism in what is being done. Based on Bradley et al. report [11], quality has three dimensions to it; the first dimension is clinical quality which focuses on the safety and appropriateness of the care provided. Clinical quality is assessed by measuring the extent of abidance to international clinical guidelines and the extent of application of evidence based medicine. Another important measure of clinical quality is mortality ratio; however this outcome measure has been extensively criticized in the literature [12]. The second dimension of quality is managerial quality which refers to the extent of support provided by the different administrative systems to ensure quality of care. This latter is assessed using balance-score cards and the availability of needed supplies and records. Last but not least is patient experience. Patient experience is an important dimension and measure of quality because healthcare is becoming centered on patient's care and satisfaction [11]. This term spans the whole journey of the continuum of care starting from the accessibility to healthcare providers to the multiple touch points along that continuum including the after service follow up [13]. In a recent study by the Beryl Institute on patient experience benchmarking, 45% of United States based hospitals and 35% on non US based hospital have different definitions for what patient experience stands for [14]. In summary it is "the sum of all interactions, shaped by an organization culture that influences patient perceptions, across the continuum of care".

That being said, we have elected in this investigation to focus on quality as an intermediate healthcare outcome measure. Quality was assessed using two questions, namely "Ability to retain patients", and "patient experience". Subjects were asked to indicate on a seven point scale, where 1 = little importance and 7 = Extreme importance, the importance their organization attaches to the below measures. They were also asked to indicate on a seven point scale, where 1 = highly dissatisfied and 7 = highly satisfied, the extent to which your organization is currently satisfied with the below measures. For each performance measure, namely "ability to retain patients" and "patient experience", a weighted average was computed by multiplying both scores, those of satisfaction and importance. For the "ability to retain patients" the weighted average score is referred to as "performance measure 1" and for "patient satisfaction" the weighted average is referred to as "performance measure 2".

8.1.1 Statistical Method

The internal consistency of the scales was assessed by calculating the Cronbach Alpha and item to total correlation for the scales (differentiation strategy and low-cost leadership) and their respective items. An alpha greater than 0.7 is an indicative of good internal consistency. These are displayed in Table 8.1.

Descriptive statistical analysis was used to report the frequency and means (mean and SD) of all the instrument's items giving a rating greater than or equal to 5 (over 7) for their responses. These are displayed in Table 8.2. Table 8.3 represents 3

Table 8.1 Scale reliability analysis

	Total sample Cronbach Alpha	Item-to-total correlation
Differentiation strategy	0.7630	
Introduce new services/centers		0.7489
Differentiate existing services		0.9045
Utilizing market research to identify new services		0.8464
Low-cost leadership	0.8590	
Achieving lower cost of services than competitors		0.6560
Making services/procedures more-cost efficient		0.8585
Improving the time and cost required for co-ordination of various services		0.8555
Improving the utilization of available staff, equipment, services and facilities		0.7519
Performing an analysis of costs associated with various services		0.8274
Improving availability of diagnostic equipment and auxiliary services to control costs		0.7056

Table 8.2 Strategy and quality of care item analysis

	Mean	SD	(Score ≥ 5)	
			N	%
Introduce new services/centers	5.6	1.2	20	83.3
Differentiate existing services	5.5	1.2	21	87.5
Utilizing market research to identify new services	4.9	1.7	14	58.3
Differentiation strategy	5.3	1.1	16	66.7
Achieving lower cost of services than competitors	5.2	1.7	16	66.7
Making services/procedures more-cost efficient	5.4	1.4	16	66.7
Improving the time and cost required for co-ordination of various services	5.3	1.5	13	54.2
Improving the utilization of available staff, equipment, services and facilities	6.0	1.2	20	83.3
Performing an analysis of costs associated with various services	5.6	1.3	21	87.5
Improving availability of diagnostic equipment and auxiliary services to control costs	5.8	1.5	20	83.3
low-cost leadership	5.6	1.1	16	66.7
Ability to retain patients (Interest)	5.9	1.2	20	83.3
Patients experience (Interest)	6	1.0	22	91.7
Ability to retain patients (Satisfaction)	5.4	1.4	19	79.2
Patients experience (Satisfaction)	5.5	1.8	20	83.3
Performance measure 1	33.4	12.2	–	–
Performance measure 2	33.6	9.6	–	–

Table 8.3 Strategy score analysis by strategy preference

	Differentiation (N = 16)		low-cost (N = 16)		Both (N = 13)	
	Mean	SD	Mean	SD	Mean	SD
Differentiation strategy	5.9	0.8	5.7	1.04	6.08	0.84
low-cost leadership	5.8	1.1	6.1	0.7	6.1	0.8
Performance measure 1	37.7	7.8	36.9	8.9	38.5	7.8
Performance measure 2	38.1	4.6	36.6	6.5	38.1	4.9

categories of respondents: (i) those who were in favor of a differentiation strategy (having a score of 5 or above), (ii) those who were in favor of a low-cost strategy (having a score of 5 or above) and those who were in favor of the differentiation and low-cost strategy at the same time (having a score of 5 or above on both). Mean scores and SD of the 4 measures (differentiation strategy, low-cost leadership, ability to retain, and patient experience) were calculated for each of the 3 groups.

Table 8.4 Cluster analysis

| | Complete | | | | | | |
| | Cluster 1 (N = 12) | | Cluster 2 (N = 6) | | Cluster 3 (N = 5) | | |
	Mean	SD	Mean	SD	Mean	SD	p-value
Differentiation strategy	5.1	0.6	6.8	0.41	4.2	0.99	0.0000
low-cost leadership	5.5	0.6	6.8	0.5	4.1	0.8	0.0000
Performance measure 1	34.6	8.7	40.2	6.5	19.4	14.7	0.0063
Performance measure 2	34.9	6.9	40	3.1	21.2	10.5	0.0009

Table 8.5 Correlations among strategy and quality scores

	Differentiation strategy	low-cost leadership	Performance measure 1	Performance measure 2
Differentiation strategy	1			
low-cost leadership	0.6866 (0.0003)	1		
Performance measure 1	0.5991 (0.0025)	0.5603 (0.0044)	1	
Performance measure 2	0.6195 (0.0016)	0.5231 (0.0087)	0.8022 (0.0000)	1

Table 8.4 represents Hierarchical cluster analysis that was used in order to unearth the different strategic types of hospitals based on their use of the differentiation strategy or the low-cost leadership one. The Kruskal-Wallis test was used to compare whether the different strategies were significantly associated with the 3 emerging clusters.

The correlation across the different strategies was assessed using Spearman correlation. P-value smaller than 0.05 was used to indicate statistical significance. These are displayed in Table 8.5.

8.2   Results

8.2.1   Demographic Data

A total of 23 have responded to the 60 questionnaires that were distributed. All the chief administrators who responded were from urban areas and the size of hospitals ranged between 17 beds to 540 beds with close to 80% being between 30 and 300 beds. No data was retrieved regarding the type of hospitals as being primary, secondary or tertiary caring hospitals because that would relate to the average duration of stay, information that was not readily available.

8.2.2 Reliability of Differentiation and Low-Cost Leadership Scales

The reliability exceeded the recommended 0.7 threshold for both scales. The item-to-total correlation ranged between 0.75 and 0.91 for the items within the differentiation strategy scale, and between 0.65 and 0.86 for the items within the low-cost leadership scale. See Table 8.1.

8.2.3 The Mean Score and Frequency Across the Differentiation Strategy Items, Low Leadership Strategy Items and Performance Measures

The level of engagement in the different competitive strategic activities was found to be high across the sample of hospitals. Table 8.2 shows that over a potential total of 7, the mean score across the differentiation strategy items was 5.3 whereas the mean score across the low-cost leadership items was 5.6. The vast majority of hospitals reported a score higher than or equal to 5 on most strategy items except for "Utilizing market research to identify new services". An equal number of hospitals have used either differentiation strategy or low-cost leadership. In fact, almost 67% of hospitals fell in that category with regard to both the differentiation strategy and the low-cost leadership items. Furthermore, over a potential total of 49, the mean score with regard to both the ability to retain patients as well as the patients experience was almost 34. See Table 8.2.

8.2.4 Strategy Score Analysis by Strategy Preference with Their Corresponding Performance Scores

Table 8.3 portrays the implemented competitive strategies as well as the quality of care across three hospitals categories: those that have a score of 5 or above on differentiation strategies, low-cost leadership, and both together. The results indicate that institutions that favored a specific strategy also scored high on the other one. In fact, institutions that had a score of 5 or above on differentiation strategies had a mean score of 5.8 on low-cost leadership strategies. Similarly, institutions that had a score of 5 or above on low-cost leadership strategies had a mean score of 5.7 on differentiation strategies. See Table 8.3.

8.2.5   Clustering Analysis

There were three cluster groups in all. The second cluster group of hospitals had the highest mean score on both types of strategies, while the third cluster groups' hospitals had the lowest mean score on both types of strategies. The hospitals clustered in the first group had an intermediate score on both strategies. This clustering effect is paralleled by the impact of these strategies on the quality of care whereby the second cluster reported the best patient experience as well as the best ability to retain patients. On the other hand, the third cluster reported the worst quality of care and the first cluster reported an intermediate quality of care. These results were all found to be significant. See Table 8.4.

8.2.6   Correlation Between Type of Strategy and Quality of Care

The results indicate that the low-cost leadership strategy was moderately and significantly (corr = 0.6866; p = 0.0003) associated with the differentiation strategy. The ability to retain patients as well as the patient experience moderately correlated with the differentiation strategy in a significant manner (corr1 = 0.5991, p1 = 0.0025; corr2 = 0.6195, p2 = 0.0016). Similarly for the low-cost leadership strategy (corr1 = 0.5603, p1 = 0.0044; corr2 = 0.5231, p2 = 0.0087). The highest correlation was found to be among the patients experience and the ability to retain patients (corr = 0.8022, p = 0.0000). See Table 8.5.

8.3   Discussion

8.3.1   Descriptive Findings

The results of the investigation led by the author on the application of Porter's strategy showed that a large percentage close to 67% used differentiation strategy in isolation or in combination with low-cost leadership as a main strategic construct in their competition with other hospitals (A score > or = 5). This was also evident in the cluster analysis which revealed three clusters among which two had a differentiation score above 5, namely cluster (n = 12) and cluster 2 (n = 6). This is in partial accordance with the results of Kumar et al. [5] where differentiation strategy in focus was used in 16%, across the board in 8%, and in combination with cost leadership in 11%, making the total of 35%. The higher percentage of Lebanese hospitals using differentiation strategy can be attributed to the fact that urban hospitals unlike rural hospitals present in the sample of Kumar et al. are more likely to use differentiation strategy. Another important factor is the stratification of his sample in terms of profit versus non-profit organization. In his study a higher percentage of for-profit hospitals pursued a differentiation strategy (45%) compared to non-profit hospitals (13%). Unfortunately this data is not available in our study given the lack of transparency and reluctance in sharing any information pertaining profit in the healthcare industry.

8.3.2 Correlation Analysis

The results of this investigation have shown moderate correlation between differentiation strategy and quality of care (r = 0.591 and 0.619 for performance measure 1 and 2 respectively), and moderate correlation between cost leadership and quality of care (r = 0.560 and 0.523 for performance measure 1 and 2 respectively). The performance of hospitals that used either type of strategy, differentiation or cost leadership, was roughly similar as shown by the weighted averages of both performance parameters in Table 8.3 (37.7 and 38.1 for the differentiation group, and 36.9 and 36.6 for the cost leadership group). What is noticeable is that hospitals that used a combination of strategies, referred to as "stuck in the middle" by Porter, outperformed those that used one of the two strategies. The weighted average performance was superior to both groups (38.5 and 38.1 respectively). This was more evident in the cluster analysis where the second group that scored the highest for both types of strategies (6.8 for both differentiation and cost leadership) had the highest performance (40.2 and 40 for performance 1 and 2). The results of this investigation showed that using cost leadership hand in hand with differentiation yield better performance in terms of quality compared to the adoption of a single strategy. More so, there was a strong correlation between the two strategies as indicated by the clustering in performance as shown in Tables 8.4 and 8.5. Those who performed well have used both strategies whereas those who had a rather poor performance ranked below average in their usage of either strategies.

Our results are in accordance with those of Hlavacka et al. in his study on "Performance applications of Porter's generic strategies in Slovak hospitals". The findings of his study indicated that hospitals stuck in the middle had superior performance compared to those that emphasized one type of strategy [4]. Further examination of the data shows that close to half of this category, namely "stuck in the middle", were hospitals between 30 and 300 beds and characterized as rural. In our investigation all hospitals were urban and 83% had more than 30 and less than 300 beds. On the other hand the results of this investigation are not in accordance with those of Kumar et al. in his analysis of performance applications of Porter's generic strategies in the United States [5]. In his study, hospitals that adopted the focused low-cost leadership performed better than those that adopted the differentiation strategy, and those that used a combination had the poorest performance. This has been attributed to the "contradiction in terms of resource commitment". Porter's view of strategy indicates that firms need to focus on either differentiation strategy or low-cost leadership in order to develop and sustain a competitive advantage. Those who use both often described as "stuck in the middle" will struggle and often fail in creating a durable competitive advantage. This typology of non- viability of those stuck in the middle has been challenged by many authors such as Miller 1992, and Gilbert and Strebel 1986 [15, 16] who have shown that using a combination strategy can be successful in certain industries.

More so, those that adopted broad-based low-cost leadership had less of a return in many of the performance measures compared to those that used focused low-cost leadership. Similarly, differentiation strategy in a focused manner had higher performance compared to broad-based differentiation, a fact that has been linked to the type of payment and changes in reimbursement policies. This has also been explained on the basis that seeking differentiation across the board and in a non-focused manner can lead to fragmentation and inefficiency in operation and return. Unfortunately the current study carries no information on the focus operational mode of the Lebanese hospitals.

References

1. Miles, R.E., Snow, C.C., Meyer, A.D. and Coleman, H.J., 1978. Organizational strategy, structure, and process. *Academy of management review*, *3*(3), pp. 546–562.
2. Hill, C.W., 1988. Differentiation versus low cost or differentiation and low cost: A contingency framework. *Academy of Management Review*, *13*(3), pp. 401–412.
3. Lamont, B.T., Marlin, D., and Hoffman, J.J., 1993. Porter's Generic Strategies, Discontinuous Environments, and Performance: A Longitudinal Study of Changing Strategies in the Hospital Industry. *Health Services Research*, 28, pp. 624–40.
4. Hlavacka, S., Bacharova, L., Rusnakova, V., Wagner, R., 2001. Performance implications of Porter's generic strategies in Slovak hospitals. *Journal of Management in Medicine*, 15(1), pp. 44–66.
5. Kumar, K., Subramanian, R., Yauger, C., 1997. Pure versus hybrid: performance implications of Porter's generic strategies. *Health Care Management Review*, 22(4), pp. 47–60.
6. Miller, D., and Friesen, P.H., 1984. *Organizations: A Quantum Vie*, Prentice-Hall: New Jersey.
7. Bradley, E. H., Pallas, S., Bashyal, C., Berman, P., Curry, L., 2010. *Developing Strategies For Improving Health Care Delivery: Guide to Concepts, Determinants, Measurements, and Intervention Design*. The World Bank 1818 H Street, NW, Washington, DC 20433: The International Bank for Reconstruction and Development. Department of Health. 2008. High Quality Care For All: NHS Next Stage Review Final Report [online]. Available at: https://www.gov.uk/government/uploads/system/uploads/attachment_data/file/228836/7432.pdf [Accessed 14 January 2015].
8. Webster's Third New International Dictionary, Unabridged, Copyright 1993 Merriam-Webster, Incorporated.
9. Agency for Healthcare Research and Quality AHRQ, n.d. A quick look at Quality. [online] Available at: http://archive.ahrq.gov/consumer/qnt/qntqlook.htm [Accessed 22 January 2014].
10. Institute of Medicine, 2001. Crossing the Quality Chasm: A New Health System for the 21st Century, National Academies Press: Washington, DC.
11. Donabedian, A., 1980. *The Definition of Quality and Approaches to Its Assessment*, Health Administration Press: Ann Arbor, MI.

12. Meterko, M., Wright. S., Lin, H., Lowy, E., Cleary, PD., 2010. Mortality among patients with acute myocardial infarction: the influences of patient-centered care and evidence-based medicine. *Health Services Research,* 45(5 Pt 1): pp. 1188–204. doi:10.1111/j.1475-6773. 2010.01138.x.
13. Feirn, A. Betts, D. Tribble, T., 2009 The patient experience: strategies and approaches for providers to achieve and maintain a competitive advantage. Deloitte LLP's Health Sciences Practice White Paper. Available from: https://www.deloitte.com/assets/DcomUnitedStates/ Local%20Assets/Documents/us_lshc_ThePatientExperience_072809.pdf. [Accessed on April 10, 2014].
14. Wolf, J.A. 2013. The patient experience: strategies and approaches for providers to achieve and maintain a competitive advantage, The Beryl Institute: Bedford, TX.
15. Miller, D. (1992). The generic strategy trap. *Journal of Business Strategy,* 13(1), pp. 37–42.
16. Gilbert, X., and Strebel, P., 1986. Developing Competitive Advantage. In: Guth W. D. ed., *The Handbook of Business Strategy,* Warner, Gorham and Lamont: New York, pp. 1986–87.

Chapter 9
Correlation Between Type of Strategy and Performance

9.1 Analysis of the Correlation Between the Types of Strategy and Performance in Lebanese Hospitals

9.1.1 Why Would Cost Leadership Correlate with Quality of Care?

Low cost leadership correlates with quality of care at different levels. In the "Guide to strategic cost transformation in hospitals and health systems" by the Health Research and Educational trust by Blake et al. in 2012 [1], strategic cost transformation has three pathways to it: A cost management plan that addresses mainly operation cost, non-labor cost, service cost, supply chain cost and so forth; a business restructuring plan that focuses on assessing the different services, their distribution and the means to optimize their corresponding allocated resources; and last but not least is the clinical transformation plan that is directed towards optimization of the utilization and process enhancement, both of which lead to improvement in quality of care. The correlation between cost leadership and quality of care is also in accordance with the readings of Michael E. Rindler in 2006 [2] on cost structure in its different dimensions. For instance in utility cost, optimizing clinical utilization is crucial in cost reduction and quality care. Over or under utilization of hospital resources can lead to waste and unnecessary usage of diagnostic and therapeutic materials, whereas optimal utilization can reduce cost by avoiding repetition, preventing unnecessary extension of hospital stay and reducing the rate of errors and complications and hence improve care.

Different strategic tools to reduce cost of clinical utilization have been described, most importantly of which is the creation of "clinical pathways". The rationale behind this latter is to reduce the variability in care, reduce the cost incurred and improve clinical practice [3].

© The Author(s) 2017
A. L. Hamdan, *Strategic Thinking in a Hospital Setting*,
SpringerBriefs in Public Health, DOI 10.1007/978-3-319-53597-5_9

These pathways act as roadmaps for the treatment of common medical conditions and reinforce good quality care. This mandates meticulous dissection of the common practices in the hospital, thorough examination of emerging opportunities and threats, and prudent alignment between physicians and the management team. Once clinical pathways have been set, these need to be endorsed and monitored closely. Rewarding abidance to the clinical pathways and addressing poor performance will reinforce their application among practitioners. Along the same line of thoughts is the method of creating two units each addressing a different group of patients which is the basis of the second principle namely "Corral Variability" referred to by Richard Bohmer in 2010 as "clinic-within-a-clinic" or "hospital-within-a-hospital" [4]. This duality in care has several challenges most important of which is the management of the interface between the two units and streamlining the services among their corresponding patients. Another dimension in cost reduction that correlates with quality of care and indirectly with patient experience is capital cost management. Capital cost is intimately linked to performance because hospitals that perform the best have access to the lowest–cost capital [1]. That is why it is Mandatory to incorporate quality management in any strategic plan for capital cost reduction quality and to be keen on choosing the right managers to do the right thing at the right time and at the right cost. Another principle in cost reduction that substantiates quality of care is "*reorganizing resources*" which means reconfiguring the infrastructure of the institution in order to deploy its resources in terms of staff, clinical information, measurements and incentives in a way to support patient care and experience. This principle emphasizes the importance of internal feedback and learning by doing as we progress in redesigning the workplace.

9.1.2   Why Would Differentiation Strategy and Quality of Care Correlate?

There are three main reasons why quality of care and particularly patient's experience as an outcome measure of quality would correlate with differentiation strategy. One is the strong association between patient experience and numerous clinical outcomes used in differentiation strategy. Patient experience correlates with mortality and morbidity ratio, length of hospital stay and infection rate, all of which are considered as tools for differentiating a hospital from its competitors [5, 6]. A second as important of a reason for the correlation between patient experience, differentiation and hybrid strategy is the Strong interplay between patient experience and organizational structure and performance, which again are dictated by the organizational strategy and are gagged by several outcome metrics. Pemberton and Richardson describe six steps in patient's experience all of which are intimately shaped by the organization performance and reflected in its differentiation strategy [7]. These include "reputation, arrival, contract, stay, treatment and after stay". Differentiation strategy can touch on any of these six steps, starting with branding, enhanced visibility, to high treatment outcome and customer after sale service.

Another venue for intersection between differentiation and quality of care is "collocation". According to Lee [8] the reform in patient care and experience mandates several key steps among which is collocation, a descriptive term for the allocation or clustering of physicians and medical staff caring for a specific population of patients. Collocation stems from the needs of patients and emphasizes the importance of redesigning organizations in ways to meet patients' rather than physicians' needs. This radical redesign in organizational structure exemplifies the link between structure, performance and patient experience and can act as a template for differentiation. Bohmer [9] in his chapter on the development and execution of healthcare delivery systems to improve patient experience speaks of "Managing the care" as a main principle. Managing care means that the primary focus of the organization structure, workflow and capacity, should be geared towards optimizing patient's care and not just maximizing the utilization of its resources. This is key if we as physicians in practice aim at applying evidence based medicine. This notion of "managing care" that aims at improving patient experience is a concept for differentiation if well cultivated in a hospital setting.

In the process of managing care we also need to realize that patients' conditions are stratified into two categories, those with uncomplicated conditions and those with complicated ones. This high and low variability in patient's condition mandates a new strategic approach that allows overriding of the standard processes of care of uncomplicated cases and thus corrals the existing variability among patients. Nevertheless, we should keep in mind that this duality in care has several challenges most important of which is the management of the interface between the two units and streamlining the services among these patients.

In a nutshell, attempts to improve patient experience can highlight gaps in the performance of medical teams. These may include flaws in processes, defects in clinical care, lack or insufficiency of skills and expertise, absence of motivation or accountability, and last but not least incongruence in delivery of services, all of which are potential avenues for differentiation. Frampton [10] illustrates two important dimensions of patient's experience, the personal encounters at the human level, and the environment in which care is delivered. Both of these dimensions are avenues for differentiation. At the human interaction level, differentiation can occur in enhancing both verbal and para-verbal communication skills of healthcare providers in order to better understand patients' complaints and to better relay medical instructions. Along this line of intersection, there are four basic emotional needs to be addressed, namely confidence, integrity, pride and passion, all of which can be attributes of service differentiation [11]. Differentiation can also be derived from patient engagement. Numerous studies have indicated that engaged patients are more likely to abide to medical instruction and adhere to treatment protocols compared to non-engaged patients. Their input in the decision making allows them to understand their current situation and comply with physicians' recommendations. As a result better medical care is delivered and clinical quality indices are raised.

Despite the differentiating importance of patient's centered care, the inherent nature of medical quest limits the possibility of achieving it. In industries other than healthcare, customers go through various steps in selecting the right product or service. The decision making process starts by problem recognition, search for information, narrowing the choices, and finally selection. This latter is often based on the attributes of the product, its price, promotion and place as reported by Porter in 1980 [12]. In healthcare specifically patients have many obstacles in their search for the best medical service to their condition [13]. One is the inherent nature of their quest, namely the intangibility of the service and the inability to qualify it before consumption. Two is the uncertainty to seek medical advice and the type of service needed. Three is about the hardship of gathering information on the different service providers, especially when many of the pertinent information are not displayed publically. Doing hospital specific research requires a lot of time and a basic knowledge of at least some of the technical or scientific nature of the services provided. Four is the uncertainty about the proper match between the services provided to the medical condition that the patient has. Last but not least is the complexity and lack of homogeneity in the definition and reporting of "good quality" in healthcare. The diversity is in the structural aspect vis-à-vis the capacity and up-to-date technology of the hospital facility, in the operations and processes of delivery of medical services and in the outcome measures used in reporting such as mortality ratio, rate of readmissions, duration of stay, patients experience and so forth [14]. In order to circumvent the inherent nature of a medical quest we need to develop educational programs for patients and families and improve the public awareness on the most common medical conditions.

References

1. Blake, J.W., Channon, B.S., Grube, M.E., Sussman, J.H. 2012. *A Guide to Strategic Cost Transformation in Hospitals and Health Systems*. Health Research and Educational Trust and Kaufman, Hall & Associates, Inc., Chicago. Available at: http://www.hpoe.org/Reports-HPOE/guide_strategic_cost_transformation_hospitals_health_systems.pdf. [Accessed on 18 January 2015].
2. Rindler, M.E, 2006.Why do Some Hospitals Fail? In: J. Davis, A. Bove, C. Underdown, eds. 2006. *Strategic Cost Reduction, Leading Your Hospital to Success,* Health Administration Press: North Franklin Street, Chicago, Ch. 3.
3. Grimshaw, J.M. and Russell, I.T., 1993. Effect of clinical guidelines on medical practice: a systematic review of rigorous evaluations. *The Lancet, 342*(8883), pp. 1317–1322.
4. Bohmer, R., 2010. Fixing Health Care on the Front Lines. In: no ed. 2011. *Harvard Business Review Fixing Health Care From Inside & Out,* Harvard Business Review Press: Boston, Massachusetts, pp. 29–48.
5. Doyle, C., Lennox, L., Bell, D., 2013. A systematic review of evidence on links between patient experience and clinical safety and effectiveness. *BMJ Open* [online]. Available at: http://bmjopen.bmj.com/content/3/1/e001570.full.pdf+html [Accessed 18 Jan 2015].
6. Isaac, T., Zaslavsky, A., Cleary P., Landon, B., 2010. The Relationship between Patients' Perception of Care and Measures of Hospital Quality and Safety. *Health Services Research,*45(4), pp. 1024–40.
7. Pemberton S, Richardson H. A Vision of the future for patient experience. Nursing Times. 2013; 109: 33–34.

8. Lee, T. H., 2010. Turning Doctors into Leaders. In: no ed. 2011. *Harvard Business Review Fixing Health Care From Inside & Out,* Harvard Business Review Press. Boston, Massachusetts, pp. 1–22.
9. Bohmer, R. (2012). The instrumental value of medical leadership. Engaging doctors in improving services. London: The Kings Fund.
10. Frampton S., 2012. Healthcare and the patient experience: Harmonizing care and environment. *Health Environments Research & Design Journal,* 5 (2): pp. 3–6.
11. Robison J., 2010. What is the "patient experience"? *Gallup Management Journal* [Online]. Available at: http://businessjournal.gallup.com/content/143258/patient-experience.aspx. 2010. [Accessed March 15, 2014].
12. Porter, M., 1980. Competitive Strategy, Free Press: New York.
13. Thomson, R. B., 1994. Review: Competition Among hospitals in the United States. *Health Policy,* 27, pp. 205–31.
14. Robinson, J. C., 1988. Hospital Quality Competition and the Economics of Imperfect Information. *The Milbank Quarterly,* 66, p. 475.

Chapter 10
Conclusion

Porter's generic strategies are applicable and viable in hospital settings in their pure and hybrid forms. Both differentiation and low cost leadership can be equally chosen by hospitals' executive managers as strategies for the development of sustainable Competitive advantage. There is invariably a significant correlation between the Types of strategies used and quality of care measured by the patient's experience score and the ability to sustain patient's loyalty. Though the adoption of either strategy can lead to a good performance, those who adopt both strategies hand in hand may outperform those that adopt one type of strategy in isolation.

To that end, what is needed is a "trade on" strategic plan with emphasis on service differentiation, cost reduction and value creation. A Trade on strategy can mitigate the rigidity in a given healthcare system, the volatility in its environment and the constraints in the payer mix when present.

In order to bolster patient centered care in a discontinuous environment a hybrid strategic plan must stem from within the institution and at the front lines where patients and health care providers meet. It must set the groundwork that ensures the drive for transformation, and set the priorities for the business and cultural transformation. This requires revamping of the clinical processes, managing the systems in the most resourceful manner, and changing the culture that supports the current organizational structures [1]. Several steps need to be taken before the implementation of Hybrid strategy and these include voicing and sharing the vision of the organization and its goals, building of uniform measurement system across the different providers in healthcare, improving processes and dismantling cultural barriers. These steps form a prelude for the implementation of hybrid type of strategy that combines cost reduction with service differentiation and radical innovation [2]. That being said, coming up with a strategic plan is only the beginning of any change within an institution. Both leaders and managers have to work together at three levels to introduce, implement and manage change. The first level is where the mission and vision of the institution needs to be revised while emphasizing the core values. This is usually accompanied by a clear strategic plan that draws the road map from point A to point B. In health care as previously mentioned the strategic plan is usually a

© The Author(s) 2017
A. L. Hamdan, *Strategic Thinking in a Hospital Setting*,
SpringerBriefs in Public Health, DOI 10.1007/978-3-319-53597-5_10

hybrid plan that covers low cost leadership and service differentiation. The second level of change is at the level of the processes and procedures, examining what needs to be revised, re-engineered, and what new technology needs to be introduced. The third level of change which is the most important is behavior of the staff, employee and subordinates in the implementation of the change. By behavior we are referring to what they say and do, which markedly impacts the success of change and the productivity of institution [3].

References

1. Bohmer, R., 2010. Fixing Health Care on the Front Lines. In: no ed. 2011. *Harvard Business Review Fixing Health Care From Inside & Out,* Harvard Business Review Press: Boston, Massachusetts, pp. 29–48.
2. Lee, T. H., 2010. Turning Doctors into Leaders. In: no ed. 2011. *Harvard Business Review Fixing Health Care From Inside & Out,* Harvard Business Review Press: Boston, Massachusetts, pp. 1–22.
3. Remillard, J., Westgate, C., 2016. Leading Change, *McGill Executive Institute.*

Index

Note: Page numbers followed by *f* and *t* indicate figures and tables respectively

© The Author(s) 2017
A. L. Hamdan, *Strategic Thinking in a Hospital Setting*,
SpringerBriefs in Public Health, DOI 10.1007/978-3-319-53597-5

Printed in the United States
By Bookmasters